SECOND EDITION

VOLUME EIGHT

John Steptoe to Charlotte Zolotow

Favorite Children's
AUTHORS *and*
ILLUSTRATORS

E. Russell Primm III, Editor in Chief

ᕈ

PO Box 326, Chanhassen, MN 55317-0326
800/599-READ
http://www.childsworld.com

A Note to Our Readers:

The publication dates listed in each author's or illustrator's selected bibliography represent the date of first publication in the United States.

The editors have listed literary awards that were announced prior to August 2006.

Every effort has been made to contact copyright holders of material included in this reference work. If any errors or omissions have occurred, corrections will be made in future editions.

Photographs: 8—James Rapiequet Aclsmidt / HarperCollins; 12, 112, 128—Harcourt; 16—Judith St. George; 20, 60, 108, 120—Scholastic; 32—John Graves / Harcourt; 40—AP Photo; 48, 104—Houghton Mifflin; 52—Random House; 64—Kurt Bomz / Houghton Mifflin; 68—Candlewick Press; 72—Albert Whitman and Company; 76, 132—Penguin Putnam; 84—Peggy Morsch / Houghton Mifflin; 88, 96, 144—HarperCollins; 92—Hyperion Books; 116—Jacqueline Woodson; 124—Joanne Ryder / HarperCollins; 136—Karen Hoyle / Kerlan Collection, University of Minnesota; 152—David Koff / Crescent Dragonwagon.

An Editorial Directions book

Library of Congress Cataloging-in-Publication Data

Favorite children's authors and illustrators / E. Russell Primm III, editor-in-chief. — 2nd ed.
   v. cm.
   Includes bibliographical references and index.
   Contents: v. 1. Verna Aardema to Ashley Bryan.
   ISBN-13: 978-1-59187-057-9 (v.1 : alk. paper)
   ISBN-10: 1-59187-057-7 (v. 1 : alk. paper)
   ISBN-13: 978-1-59187-058-6 (v. 2 : alk. paper)
   ISBN-10: 1-59187-058-5 (v. 2 : alk. paper)
   ISBN-13: 978-1-59187-059-3 (v. 3 : alk. paper)
   ISBN-10: 1-59187-059-3 (v. 3 : alk. paper)
   ISBN-13: 978-1-59187-060-9 (v. 4 : alk. paper)
   ISBN-10: 1-59187-060-7 (v. 4 : alk. paper)
   ISBN-13: 978-1-59187-061-6 (v. 5 : alk. paper)
   ISBN-10: 1-59187-061-5 (v. 5 : alk. paper)
   ISBN-13: 978-1-59187-062-3 (v. 6 : alk. paper)
   ISBN-10: 1-59187-062-3 (v. 6 : alk. paper)
   ISBN-13: 978-1-59187-063-0 (v. 7 : alk. paper)
   ISBN-10: 1-59187-063-1 (v. 7 : alk. paper)
   ISBN-13: 978-1-59187-064-7 (v. 8 : alk. paper)
   ISBN-10: 1-59187-064-X (v. 8 : alk. paper)
   1. Children's literature—Bio-bibliography—Dictionaries—Juvenile literature. 2. Young adult literature Bio-bibliography—Dictionaries—Juvenile literature. 3. Illustrators—Biography—Dictionaries—Juvenile literature. 4. Children—Books and reading—Dictionaries—Juvenile literature. 5. Young Adults—Books and reading—Dictionaries—Juvenile literature. I. Primm, E. Russell, 1958–
   PN1009.A1F38 2007
   809'.8928203—dc22
   [B]   2006011358

First printing.

Table of Contents

MAJOR CHILDREN'S AUTHOR AND ILLUSTRATOR LITERARY AWARDS

THE AMERICAN BOOK AWARDS
Awarded from 1980 to 1983 in place of the National Book Award to give national recognition to achievement in several categories of children's literature

THE BOSTON GLOBE–HORN BOOK AWARDS
Established in 1967 by Horn Book *magazine and the* Boston Globe *newspaper to honor the year's best fiction, poetry, nonfiction, and picture books for children*

THE CALDECOTT MEDAL
Established in 1938 and presented by the Association for Library Service to Children division of the American Library Association to illustrators for the most distinguished picture book for children from the preceding year

THE CARNEGIE MEDAL
Established in 1936 and presented by the British Library Association for an outstanding book for children written in English

THE CARTER G. WOODSON BOOK AWARDS
Established in 1974 and presented by the National Council for the Social Studies for the most distinguished social science books appropriate for young readers that depict ethnicity in the United States

THE CORETTA SCOTT KING AWARDS
Established in 1970 in connection with the American Library Association to honor African American authors and illustrators whose books are deemed outstanding, educational, and inspirational

THE HANS CHRISTIAN ANDERSEN MEDAL
Established in 1956 by the International Board on Books for Young People to honor an author or illustrator, living at the time of nomination, whose complete works have made a lasting contribution to children's literature

THE KATE GREENAWAY MEDAL

Established by the Youth Libraries Group of the British Library Association in 1956 to honor illustrators of children's books published in the United Kingdom

THE LAURA INGALLS WILDER AWARD

Established by the Association for Library Service to Children division of the American Library Association in 1954 to honor an author or illustrator whose books, published in the United States, have made a substantial and lasting contribution to children's literature

THE MICHAEL L. PRINTZ AWARD

Established by the Young Adult Library Services division of the American Library Association in 2000 to honor literary excellence in young adult literature (fiction, nonfiction, poetry, or anthology)

THE NATIONAL BOOK AWARDS

Established in 1950 to give national recognition to achievement in fiction, nonfiction, poetry, and young people's literature

THE NEWBERY MEDAL

Established in 1922 and presented by the Association for Library Service to Children division of the American Library Association for the most distinguished contribution to children's literature in the preceding year

THE ORBIS PICTUS AWARD FOR OUTSTANDING NONFICTION

Established in 1990 by the National Council of Teachers of English to honor an outstanding informational book published in the preceding year

THE PURA BELPRÉ AWARD

Established in 1996 and cosponsored by the Association for Library Service to Children division of the American Library Association and the National Association to Promote Library Services to the Spanish Speaking to recognize a writer and illustrator of Latino or Latina background whose works affirm and celebrate the Latino experience

THE SCOTT O'DELL AWARD

Established in 1982 and presented by the O'Dell Award Committee to an American author who writes an outstanding tale of historical fiction for children or young adults that takes place in the New World

John Steptoe

Born: September 14, 1950
Died: August 28, 1989

John Steptoe once said that the two greatest forces that shaped him were the outside world of New York City's streets and the inner world of his imagination. When he was sixteen years old, he combined these two worlds into the creation of a picture book entitled *Stevie.* It was published two years later in 1969. *Stevie* is about a boy named Robert trying to cope with the arrival of Stevie, a neighbor's child whom Robert's mother has agreed to look after. The remarkable thing about *Stevie* is that the characters speak the language that John Steptoe spoke growing up. The words are spelled out just as they would be

---

JOHN STEPTOE WON ACCLAIM FOR HIS ADAPTATIONS OF NATIVE AMERICAN AND AFRICAN AMERICAN FOLKTALES IN *THE STORY OF JUMPING MOUSE: A NATIVE AMERICAN LEGEND* AND *MUFARO'S BEAUTIFUL DAUGHTERS: AN AFRICAN TALE.*

pronounced by black kids in the Bedford-Stuyvesant section of Brooklyn, New York, where Steptoe was raised. This style of writing in realistic dialogue had never really been done before.

John Steptoe was born on September 14, 1950, in Brooklyn. John was the oldest of four children. His father was a transit worker in New York City's subway system.

As a child, John Steptoe was amazed that no one in children's books spoke the way he did. The vast majority of African American children, he felt, were being ignored as readers.

> *"Good books are more than a luxury; they are a necessary part of a child's development and it's all of our jobs to see that we all get them."*

John Steptoe started out as a painter, not a writer. He drew in the quiet of his home, while outside horns blared and throngs of people passed by. His talent won him a place at the High School of Art and Design in Manhattan. Just three months shy of finishing, he left school and New York, and started hitchhiking.

The hitchhiking didn't really lead anywhere, so Steptoe sent some of his pictures to New York publishers. *Stevie* was the result. After that, he produced many books that critics praised for their originality and for

JOHN STEPTOE'S COURAGE TO WRITE ABOUT SERIOUS THEMES FOR CHILDREN WON HIM MUCH ATTENTION. IN *DADDY IS A MONSTER . . . SOMETIMES,* HE WRITES ABOUT DOMESTIC PROBLEMS.

A Selected Bibliography of Steptoe's Work

Baby Says (1988)

Mufaro's Beautiful Daughters: An African Tale (1987)

The Story of Jumping Mouse: A Native American Legend (1984)

All the Colors of the Race: Poems (Illustrations only, 1982)

OUTside INside Poems (Illustrations only, 1981)

Mother Crocodile = Maman-Caïman (Illustrations only, 1981)

Daddy Is a Monster . . . Sometimes (1980)

She Come Bringing Me That Little Baby Girl (1974)

Train Ride (1971)

Uptown (1970)

Stevie (1969)

Steptoe's Major Literary Awards

1988 Caldecott Honor Book

1988 Coretta Scott King Illustrator Award

1987 Boston Globe-Horn Book Picture Book Award
  Mufaro's Beautiful Daughters: An African Tale

1985 Caldecott Honor Book
  The Story of Jumping Mouse: A Native American Legend

1983 Coretta Scott King Illustrator Honor Book
  All the Colors of the Race: Poems

1982 Coretta Scott King Illustrator Award
  Mother Crocodile = Maman-Caïman

1975 Boston Globe-Horn Book Picture Book Honor Book
  She Come Bringing Me That Little Baby Girl

taking on tough subjects. In *Train Ride,* for example, Steptoe depicts two young kids riding on the subway talking about what they want when they grow up. His drawings of the city include the graffiti that once decorated New York's subways. The children use the words of African American city children, but the story is universal.

John Steptoe died on August 28, 1989, from AIDS-related complications. He was

"One of my incentives for getting into writing children's books was the great and disastrous need for books that black children could honestly relate to."

thirty-eight years old. Steptoe left behind a daughter, Bweela, and a son, Javaka. Javaka Steptoe followed in his father's footsteps by becoming a Coretta Scott King Award–winning illustrator.

❧

WHERE TO FIND OUT MORE ABOUT JOHN STEPTOE

BOOKS
Berg, Julie. *John Steptoe: The Young at Heart.*
Edina, Minn.: Abdo & Daughters, 1994.

De Montveville, Doris, and Elizabeth D. Crawford, eds.
Fourth Book of Junior Authors & Illustrators.
New York: H. W. Wilson Company, 1978.

Kovacs, Deborah, and James Preller. *Meet the Authors and Illustrators:
60 Creators of Favorite Children's Books Talk about Their Work.* Vol. 1.
New York: Scholastic, 1991.

McElmeel, Sharron L. *100 Most Popular Picture Book Authors and Illustrators: Biographical
Sketches and Bibliographies.* Englewood, Colo.: Libraries Unlimited, 2000.

Silvey, Anita, ed. *The Essential Guide to Children's Books and Their Creators.*
Boston: Houghton Mifflin Company, 2002.

WEB SITES
AUTHOR TRACKER
http://www.authortracker.com/author.asp?a=authorid&b=12770
For biographical information and a list of works

HARPER CHILDRENS BOOKS
http://www.harperchildrens.com/teacher/catalog/author_xml.asp?authorID=12770
For biographical information about John Steptoe

———

IN 1989, JOHN STEPTOE'S *MUFARO'S BEAUTIFUL DAUGHTERS: AN
AFRICAN TALE* WAS MADE INTO A MOTION PICTURE.

Janet Stevens

Born: January 17, 1953

Picture book author and illustrator Janet Stevens is a hit with kids and teachers alike. Kids love her zany, colorful drawings. In Stevens's books, readers might meet a bear in a Hawaiian shirt, a walrus in a tie, or an elephant in a tutu. Teachers love Stevens's work, too. They know that her wild and wacky illustrations excite kids and make them want to read.

Janet Stevens was born on January 17, 1953, in Dallas, Texas. She is the youngest of three kids. Her older brother and sister were good students in school, but Janet preferred to draw. In class, she doodled on all of her papers. Instead of writing book reports, she drew them. Janet's parents nicknamed her "the artist."

In high school, Janet drew pictures for anything and anybody. She designed posters and yearbook covers. At the University of Colorado, she

---

SOME OF STEVENS'S FAVORITE THINGS TO DRAW ARE SHOES WITH HIGH HEELS. SHE ALSO LIKES TO DRAW RHINOCEROSES, BEARS, PIGS, AND CATS.

majored in art. During summer breaks, she flew to Honolulu and designed patterns for Hawaiian shirts! When Stevens graduated in 1975, she knew without a doubt that she wanted to be an artist.

In 1978, Stevens got her first job working on a children's book. That book was *Callooh! Callay! Holiday Poems for Young Readers.* Since then, Stevens has worked full-time making books for kids. Sometimes she creates drawings for other people's books. She tries to put the author's vision into pictures. At other times, Stevens writes her own books or retells classic fables or fairy tales. When Stevens is working on her own book, she can let her imagination run wild.

A Selected Bibliography of Stevens's Work

Great Fuzz Frenzy (with Susan Stevens Crummel, 2005)

Why Epossumondas Has No Hair on His Tail (Illustrations only, 2004)

Jackalope (with Susan Stevens Crummel, 2003)

Epossumondas (Illustrations only, 2002)

Tumbleweed Stew (Illustrations only, 2000)

And the Dish Ran Away with the Spoon (with Susan Stevens Crummel, 2001)

Cook-a-Doodle-Doo! (with Susan Stevens Crummel, 1999)

My Big Dog (with Susan Stevens Crummel, 1999)

Shoe Town (with Susan Stevens Crummel, 1999)

To Market! To Market! (Illustrations only, 1997)

Tops & Bottoms (1995)

Anansi and the Talking Melon (Illustrations only, 1994)

Coyote Steals the Blanket: An Ute Tale (1993)

Anansi Goes Fishing (Illustrations only, 1992)

The Dog Who Had Kittens (Illustrations only, 1991)

How the Manx Cat Lost Its Tail (1990)

Anansi and the Moss-Covered Rock (Illustrations only, 1988)

The Three Billy Goats Gruff (1987)

The Tortoise and the Hare: An Aesop Fable (1984)

The Princess and the Pea (1982)

Lucretia the Unbearable (Illustrations only, 1981)

Callooh! Callay! Holiday Poems for Young Readers (Illustrations only, 1978)

Stevens's Major Literary Awards

1996 Caldecott Honor Book
Tops & Bottoms

> *"Each book is an opportunity and a challenge. A new book offers me a chance to expand and try something new. The process is both difficult and exciting—sometimes a struggle, sometimes fun. Most important is to create books that children want to read. This is the real joy of bookmaking."*

Stevens is always looking for new ways to create art. In the past, she has used colored pencils, watercolors, and acrylic paints, as well as photo and fabric collages. Most recently, Stevens has begun creating art with her computer. She uses a scanner to take pictures of household items and store them in her computer. In *My Big Dog,* Stevens scanned in some cloth and buttons. Then she used the images of these items in her artwork.

Stevens's drawing style has also evolved over the years. She visits classrooms around the country and talks to kids about what they like to see. Stevens uses their comments to improve her work.

Stevens likes to include people she knows in her books. Her friends, family,

> *"Jump into a book like a cool swimming pool on a hot summer day, and feel it all around you. Read at your own pace. Reread the parts you don't get—or that you like the most. Dive into it! Become the character in the book; feel all the feelings."*

STEVENS AND HER SISTER, SUSAN STEVENS CRUMMEL, HAVE WRITTEN A NUMBER OF CHILDREN'S BOOKS TOGETHER, INCLUDING *AND THE DISH RAN AWAY WITH THE SPOON,* *COOK-A-DOODLE-DOO!,* *MY BIG DOG,* AND *SHOE TOWN.*

and pets have all posed for her pictures. She also likes to draws things like furniture and shoes that are in her house. In *To Market! To Market!* Janet used the local grocery store as a model.

Janet Stevens lives in Boulder, Colorado, with her husband, son, daughter, three cats, and a dog. Stevens's two children are important to her work. They look at her books and tell her what they think. Stevens always tries to create drawings that her kids will enjoy, and she has certainly been successful.

&

WHERE TO FIND OUT MORE ABOUT JANET STEVENS

BOOKS

Holtze, Sally Holmes, ed. *Sixth Book of Junior Authors & Illustrators.*
New York: H .W. Wilson Company, 1989.

McElmeel, Sharron L. *100 Most Popular Picture Book Authors and Illustrators: Biographical Sketches and Bibliographies.* Englewood, Colo.: Libraries Unlimited, 2000.

WEB SITES

JANET STEVENS HOME PAGE
http://www.janetstevens.com/
For information about Janet Stevens's life and work

MEET JANET STEVENS
http://www.scottforesman.com/families/authors/stevens.html
To read an interview with Stevens

WHEN JANET STEVENS WAS A CHILD, HER FATHER WAS IN THE NAVY, SO THE FAMILY MOVED AROUND A LOT. STEVENS HAS LIVED IN TEXAS, MASSACHUSETTS, MAINE, VIRGINIA, RHODE ISLAND, FLORIDA, HAWAII, GEORGIA, AND COLORADO.

Judith St. George

Born: February 26, 1931

Judith St. George loves to make history come alive. She is the author of more than forty books for young people. Many of them are historical novels, and several are inspired by her own experiences.

The author was born Judith Alexander in Westfield, New Jersey, in 1931. As a child, Judith was a tomboy. She was proud to be the only girl on the local boys' baseball team. In the winter, she enjoyed sledding down the snowbanks and skating on a frozen pond.

Judith loved to read. Every Saturday morning, she rode her bike to the little brick Westfield Public Library. Often, she couldn't wait to get home to begin reading her books. She'd stop by a favorite tree, climb up into its branches, and read there.

ST. GEORGE CREATED AN EDUCATIONAL PACKET ABOUT THE BROOKLYN BRIDGE FOR NEW YORK CITY SCHOOLCHILDREN.

Among Judith's favorite books were mysteries. She liked the Wizard of Oz books, as well. "I also had the best comic book collection in the neighborhood," she recalls. Judith tried her hand at writing, too. She wrote a play in sixth grade, and she and her friends performed it in the school auditorium.

At Smith College in Northampton, Massachusetts, she took every available creative writing course. After graduation in 1952, she worked for a steamship company in New York City. In 1954, she married David St. George, an Episcopal minister. At first, the couple lived in the Longfellow House in Cambridge, Massachusetts. George Washington had made his headquarters there during part of the Revolutionary War (1775–1783). Living here gave the young bride an exciting connection with history.

"I'm a library freak, and for me, there's nothing like the high I get when I walk through the doors of a library, any library."

In time, the family grew to include four children—Peter, James, Philip, and Sarah. Once her three oldest children were in school, St. George began thinking about writing a book. At that time, the family home was close to Jockey Hollow, an area near Morristown, New Jersey. American troops had camped there during the Revolutionary War. St. George decided to write a spy story set in Jockey Hollow during the

ST. GEORGE WAS APPOINTED AS NEW JERSEY'S DELEGATE TO THE WHITE HOUSE CONFERENCE ON LIBRARIES AND INFORMATION SERVICES IN 1979.

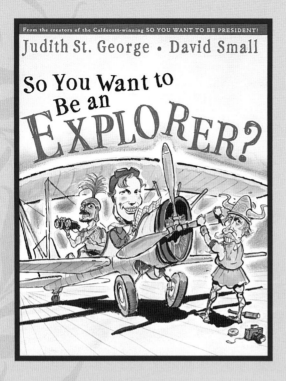

From the creators of the Caldecott-winning SO YOU WANT TO BE PRESIDENT!

Judith St. George • David Small

So You Want to Be an EXPLORER?

A Selected Bibliography of St. George's Work

Make Your Mark, Franklin Roosevelt! (2007)

So You Want to Be President? (2000)

Crazy Horse (1994)

The White House: Cornerstone of a Nation (1990)

The Panama Canal: Gateway to the World (1989)

What's Happening to My Junior Year? (1986)

The Mount Rushmore Story (1985)

In the Shadow of the Bear (1983)

Do You See What I See? (1982)

The Brooklyn Bridge: They Said It Couldn't Be Built (1982)

Call Me Margo (1981)

Haunted (1980)

The Halloween Pumpkin Smasher (1978)

By George, Bloomers! (1976)

Turncoat Winter, Rebel Spring (1970)

war. After nine rejections, *Turncoat Winter, Rebel Spring* was finally published in 1970.

More than forty books followed over the years. Many of St. George's stories are historical fiction, while others are historical nonfiction. She always researches her subjects thoroughly. "To my surprise," she recalls, "I found that doing research was the most fun of all."

In 1983, New York City celebrated the centennial, or one hundredth anniversary, of its famous Brooklyn Bridge. St. George was asked to help

"People always comment on how hard the research must be, but I tell them that it's the research that's fun."

plan the celebration by serving on the Brooklyn Bridge Centennial Commission. This inspired her to write *The Brooklyn Bridge: They Said It Couldn't Be Built*.

The St. Georges loved to travel, and they visited Europe, Russia, Canada, and Alaska. They went to Panama when St. George was writing *The Panama Canal: Gateway to the World*. At one point during the trip, she had the scary experience of climbing a rope ladder from one boat to another in the dark of night. For St. George, it was just another research adventure.

Today, St. George lives in Old Lyme, Connecticut.

⚬

WHERE TO FIND OUT MORE ABOUT JUDITH ST. GEORGE

BOOK
Holtze, Sally Holmes, ed. *Sixth Book of Junior Authors and Illustrators.*
New York: H. W. Wilson, 1989.

WEB SITE
JUDITH ST. GEORGE HOME PAGE
http://www.judithstgeorge.com/
For a biography, a listing of her books, and a way to contact the author

―――――

AS A CHILD, JUDITH ENJOYED HISTORICAL NOVELS SUCH AS CAROL R. BRINK'S *CADDIE WOODLAWN* AND RACHEL FIELD'S *HITTY: HER FIRST HUNDRED YEARS.*

R. L. Stine

Born: October 8, 1943

The writer most young readers think of when they think of scary books is R. L. Stine. But he is about as scary your local librarian. Far from having any ghoulish qualities, Stine is as friendly a guy as you'll ever meet. Just don't read his books if you're all alone in the house.

Robert Laurence Stine was born on October 8, 1943, in Columbus, Ohio. As a child, Stine read a great deal of science fiction. His favorite authors were Ray Bradbury and Isaac Asimov. He also loved old horror movies, as well as *MAD* magazine, and the comic books *Tales from the Crypt* and *The Vault of Horror*. These comics were both funny and scary at the same time. They would one day influence Stine's writing in the Goosebumps series.

WHAT SCARES R. L. STINE THE MOST? JUMPING INTO A SWIMMING POOL.
ALTHOUGH HE CAN SWIM, HE SAYS HE HAS TO CLIMB, NOT JUMP, TO GET IN.

R. L. Stine began writing at the age of nine. Using an old type-writer, he wrote joke books and short stories, and created his own magazines. He handed them out to his fellow students, much to the unhappiness of his teachers.

It was not until high school that R. L. Stine's teachers encouraged his writing, directing him to the high school newspaper, for which he wrote a regular humor column. After graduating from high school, Stine attended Ohio State University, where he was editor of the university's humor magazine, the *Sundial.*

Following college, he moved to New York City where he worked as a writer on books, magazines, and even a Nickelodeon television show called *Eureka's Castle.* Writing under the name Jovial Bob Stine, he wrote humor books such as *101 Silly Monster Jokes* and *Bozos on Patrol,* and he was the editor in chief of *Bananas,* a humor magazine for children.

In 1986 Stine wrote *Blind Date,* his first scary novel for teenagers. This was such a big hit that a few years later he began writing the Fear Street series of scary books for teenagers.

> *"I've liked scary stuff since I was a kid. My brother and I used to go to every scary movie that came out. We saw movies like* **It Came from beneath the Sea** *and* **The Creature from the Black Lagoon.** *I remember these . . . when I think up titles for Goosebumps."*

R. L. STINE HAS HIS OWN PINBALL MACHINE AND POOL TABLE IN HIS APARTMENT IN NEW YORK CITY. THEY HELP HIM RELAX FOLLOWING A HARD DAY OF WRITING.

Bad dog. Really BAD dog.

THE BARKING GHOST

SCHOLASTIC

A Selected Bibliography of Stine's Work

Dudes, the School Is Haunted! (2006)

Freaks and Shrieks (2005)

Dangerous Girls: The Taste of Night (2004)

Dare (2004)

Beware! R. L. Stine Picks His Favorite Scary Stories (2002)

The Howler (2001)

Dear Diary, I'm Dead (2000)

Locker 13 (2000)

Don't Forget Me! (2000)

Into the Twister of Terror (1999)

The Werewolf in the Living Room (1999)

Nightmare Hour (1999)

Fear Hall, the Beginning (1997)

The Girl Who Cried Monster (1997)

Go to Your Tomb—Right Now! (1997)

Beware of the Purple Peanut Butter (1996)

A Shocker on Shock Street (1995)

The New Boy (1994)

The Scarecrow Walks at Midnight (1994)

The Haunted Mask (1993)

The Secret (1993)

Be Careful What You Wish For . . . (1993)

Bozos on Patrol (1992)

Say Cheese and Die! (1992)

The Best Friend (1992)

Blind Date (1986)

101 Silly Monster Jokes (1986)

Then, in 1992, Stine launched Goosebumps, a new series of scary books for younger readers, ages eight to twelve. It went on to become the best-selling series of all time. Young readers loved the combination of horror and humor. The series, which still runs, has sold more than 200 million books and has been translated into sixteen languages in thirty-one countries.

Goosebumps became a successful TV series, but Stine never stopped writing books. (Working six days a week, Stine writes a new Goosebumps book and a new Fear Street book each month.) He has written one scary book for adults called *Superstitious,* but he says that he prefers writing for young readers.

R. L. Stine is proud that his writing has inspired many young people, especially boys who were not previously readers, to pick up books. He is dedicated to literacy for kids and has established a writing program in the middle schools of his hometown, Columbus, Ohio. This "scary" writer with a sharp sense of humor says that on his tombstone he wants the words: "He got boys to read."

> *"My advice is to read, read, read. And don't just read me, read all kinds of authors. That way, you pick up a lot of different writing styles. . . . If you're really serious about writing, you should write something every day, even if it's just a paragraph."*

WHERE TO FIND OUT MORE ABOUT R. L. STINE

BOOKS

Meister, Cari. *R. L. Stine*. Edina, Minn.: Abdo & Daughters, 2002.

Stine, R. L., and Joe Arthur. *It Came from Ohio: My Life As a Writer*. New York: Scholastic, 1997.

WEB SITES

GOOSEBUMPS
http://www.scholastic.com/goosebumps/
To learn more about the Goosebumps series

R.L. STINE HOME PAGE
http://www.rlstine.com/
For information about the author, his works and games.

SOMETHING WICKED THIS WAY COMES BY SCIENCE-FICTION GREAT RAY BRADBURY IS STINE'S FAVORITE SCARY BOOK. HE CALLS IT THE MOST FRIGHTENING BOOK HE'S EVER READ!

Mildred D. Taylor

Born: September 13, 1943

Mildred D. Taylor noticed something odd about the children's books that she read as a child: No one looked like her. African Americans were absent from the books she read. Even at school when she learned about slavery and the history of black America, she wondered where the heroes were. Were there no blacks who stood up for their rights? Were there no black families full of love and compassion?

Of course there were, and Mildred Taylor spent a good part of her career writing about one such African American family called the Logans. Taylor depicts the same humor and struggles that all families go through in her Logan stories. But she also captures the unique struggle of growing up black in America.

IN 1978, MILDRED D. TAYLOR'S *ROLL OF THUNDER, HEAR MY CRY* WAS PRODUCED AS A MINISERIES FOR ABC TELEVISION. THE BOOK ALSO WON A NEWBERY MEDAL IN 1977.

Mildred Taylor was born in Jackson, Mississippi, on September 13, 1943, at a time when open hatred of blacks could be found all over America. Prejudice was written into the law. In the South, blacks lived a separate existence from whites. They rode in different sections of the bus and dined in different restaurants. Blacks feared a run-in with the law because the police did not treat them fairly.

"When we children had finished all the games we could think to play, we would join the adults . . . for it would often turn to . . . a history of black people told through stories."

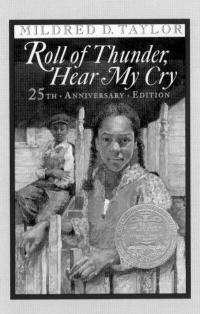

A Selected Bibliography of Taylor's Work

The Land (2001)
Mississippi Bridge (1990)
The Road to Memphis (1990)
The Friendship (1987)
The Gold Cadillac (1987)
Let the Circle Be Unbroken (1981)
Roll of Thunder, Hear My Cry (1976)
Song of the Trees (1975)

Taylor's Major Literary Awards

2002 Coretta Scott King Author Award
2002 Scott O'Dell Award
   The Land

1991 Coretta Scott King Author Award
   The Road to Memphis

1988 Boston Globe-Horn Book Fiction Award
1988 Coretta Scott King Author Award
   The Friendship

1982 Coretta Scott King Author Award
   Let the Circle Be Unbroken

1977 Boston Globe-Horn Book Fiction Honor Book
1977 Newbery Medal
   Roll of Thunder, Hear My Cry

When African American history was mentioned in class, Mildred found it to be a sad tale. Blacks were represented as helpless victims of slavery and prejudice. They somehow didn't come across as humans, with regular feelings and pride in their history.

Taylor attended college in Toledo, Ohio. She later earned a master's degree in journalism at the University of Colorado. Taylor attended school in the 1960s, when black students were fighting to end racist laws.

Taylor's interest in black history led her to work in Ethiopia as a Peace Corps volunteer. For two years, she taught English and history. When she returned to the United States in 1967, she trained other Peace Corps recruits.

> *"It is my hope that to the children who read my books, the Logans will provide those heroes missing from the schoolbooks of my childhood, Black men, women, and children of whom they can be proud."*

After moving to Los Angeles in 1971, Taylor started a novel about a black family in the South during the Great Depression. When she finished writing *Song of the Trees,* Taylor submitted it to the Council of Interracial Books for Children in 1974—and won first prize!

Since then, Mildred D. Taylor has written several novels about the Logans, including *Roll of Thunder, Hear My Cry,* which won a Newbery Medal. Taylor's books capture the struggle for dignity in a

---

TAYLOR HAS CALLED HER FATHER A "MASTER STORYTELLER." IN FACT, SHE INCLUDED MANY OF HER FAMILY'S REAL-LIFE STORIES IN HER NOVELS.

country that proclaimed equality—but only for whites. In Taylor's world, the struggle is always dignified, and being African American is something to be proud of.

Mildred D. Taylor lives in Colorado. She continues to write novels for young people.

❧

WHERE TO FIND OUT MORE ABOUT MILDRED D. TAYLOR

BOOKS

Crowe, Chris. *Presenting Mildred Taylor.*
New York: Twayne Publications, 1999.

Drew, Bernard A. *The 100 Most Popular Young Adult Authors.*
Englewood, Colo.: Libraries Unlimited, 1997

Kovacs, Deborah, and James Preller. *Meet the Authors and Illustrators:
60 Creators of Favorite Children's Books Talk about Their Work.* Vol. 1.
New York: Scholastic, 1991.

Rediger, Pat. *Great African Americans in Literature.*
New York: Crabtree, 1996.

WEB SITES

THE MISSISSIPPI WRITERS PAGE
http://www.olemiss.edu/mwp/dir/taylor_mildred/
For biographical information about Mildred D. Taylor

PENGUIN BOOKS
http://us.penguingroup.com/nf/Author/AuthorPage/0,,0_1000031974,00.html
For autobiographical information about the author

MILDRED D. TAYLOR'S MIDDLE NAME—AND FAMILY NICKNAME—IS DELOIS.

Sydney Taylor

Born: 1904
Died: February 12, 1978

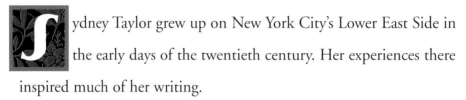

ydney Taylor grew up on New York City's Lower East Side in the early days of the twentieth century. Her experiences there inspired much of her writing.

She was born in 1904 to an immigrant Jewish family, the middle daughter of six children—five girls and one boy. In those days, the crowded tenement houses of the Lower East Side were filled with immigrants. Taylor later called it "in many ways an extension of the ghettos in middle Europe." It was a hard but exciting place to grow up. Taylor said that though the neighborhood was

"When I was a little girl and people asked, 'What would you like to be when you grow up?' I used to answer, 'An author.' But when I grew up, life had so many other attractions, I forgot about my first ambition."

filled with poverty, sickness, hard work, and long hours, it also had the joy of freedom and opportunity.

THE FIVE ALL-OF-A-KIND FAMILY STORIES ALL TAKE PLACE DURING FIVE YEARS IN THE EARLY TWENTIETH CENTURY. BUT IT TOOK TAYLOR MORE THAN TWENTY-FIVE YEARS TO WRITE THEM ALL.

Though Sydney and her family were poor, she knew they were lucky. Most families near them lived in five-story tenement buildings with no elevators and no hot water or heat. Sydney's family lived in a two-story house. And though their apartment still didn't have heat, they had their own bathroom and didn't have to share it with other families.

Taylor went to New York University, which was not far from her home. She studied drama. After graduating, she got a job as a secretary and spent her evenings working as an actress with a theater troupe called the Lenox Hill Players. She had a moment of glory with the group—one time the leading lady got sick and Taylor got to

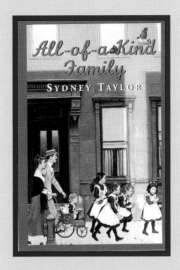

A Selected Bibliography of Taylor's Work

Danny Loves a Holiday (1980)
Ella of All-of-a-Kind Family (1978)
All-of-a-Kind Family Downtown (1972)
A Papa Like Everyone Else (1966)
The Dog Who Came to Dinner (1966)
Mr. Barney's Beard (1961)
All-of-a-Kind Family Uptown (1958)
More All-of-a-Kind Family (1954)
All-of-a-Kind Family (1951)

play her part for two nights on Broadway. As part of her work with the theater, Taylor learned to dance. She became interested in dancing and performed in the Martha Graham Dance Company from 1930 to 1935.

Taylor got married in 1925 and had a daughter named Jo. "Jo, being an only child, would listen avidly as I'd tell her about my mama, papa, and the five little sisters who lived on New York's Lower East Side," Taylor recalled later. "In the retelling, I suddenly felt a great compulsion to write it all down." That story was filled with the details of life at the turn of the century. Taylor remembered the Jewish customs and the Yiddish phrases she used to hear. She put it all on paper and let Jo and her friends read it. Then she lost interest. She stuck the story in a box and forgot about it.

Her husband didn't forget it. Starting in the 1940s, Taylor spent the summers teaching drama and dance at a camp. One summer while Taylor was gone, her husband got the story out and entered it in a contest for children's books. When Taylor returned, she got a big surprise.

> *"Our family was but a drop in the stream of bustling excitement and riotous color of the East Side of my memory. Immigrants from many lands poured into its narrow streets, bringing with them their firm beliefs in their destiny, their love of family, their great respect for learning, and . . . their hope for a better future in America."*

TAYLOR RARELY TESTED HER IDEAS OUT ON CHILDREN. "I FEEL THEY ARE IMPRESSED TOO MUCH BY ONE'S MANNER OR PRESENTATION," SHE EXPLAINED.

An editor at Follett Books contacted her, telling her she had won and asking to publish the story!

That book, *All-of-a-Kind Family,* was published in 1951. It was successful and became the first of a series that included *More All-of-a-Kind Family, All-of-a-Kind Family Uptown, All-of-a-Kind Family Downtown,* and *Ella of All-of-a-Kind Family.* She also wrote several books for very young readers. Sydney Taylor died on February 12, 1978.

❧

WHERE TO FIND OUT MORE ABOUT SYDNEY TAYLOR

BOOKS

Fuller, Muriel, ed. *More Junior Authors.*
New York: H. W. Wilson Company, 1963.

Silvey, Anita, ed. *The Essential Guide to Children's Books and Their Creators.*
Boston: Houghton Mifflin Company, 2002.

WEB SITES

LOGANBERRY BOOKS
http://www.logan.com/loganberry/most-taylor.html
For a selection of Taylor's books

THE SYDNEY TAYLOR BOOK AWARD
http://www.jewishlibraries.org/ajlweb/awards/st_books.htm
To learn more about the award established in Taylor's name

―――

AFTER TAYLOR DIED IN 1978, HER HUSBAND STARTED AN AWARD
IN HER NAME FOR THE BEST JEWISH CHILDREN'S FICTION. THE AWARD IS
STILL GIVEN BY THE ASSOCIATION OF JEWISH LIBRARIES.

Theodore Taylor

Born: June 23, 1921

Theodore Taylor writes fast-paced, action-packed tales for children and young adults. His own adventures in wartime and at sea laid the groundwork for many of his books.

Theodore Taylor was born in Statesville, North Carolina, in 1921. He grew up with four older sisters, and his family called him Ted. Ted loved to explore the fields and creeks around his home. He was an enthusiastic tree-climber, too. Money was scarce for the Taylors as Ted was growing up, and he did his part to help out. At age nine, he would get up at 4:30 in the morning to deliver newspapers before school.

Ted's first reading material was an illustrated children's edition of the Bible. He loved its "action" stories, such as the tales of David and Goliath and Daniel in the lions' den. Later, his sister Mary introduced him to the

---

TAYLOR WRITES SEVEN DAYS A WEEK, EXCEPT DURING FOOTBALL SEASON. THEN HE TAKES WEEKENDS OFF FROM WRITING.

writings of Ernest Hemingway, whose adventure and war stories excited the boy's imagination. Military history was a favorite subject for Ted. In school, he often drew pictures of warplanes and cannons in his notebooks.

When Ted was thirteen, his family moved to Portsmouth, Virginia. There Ted got a job as a cub reporter (a kind of apprentice) for the *Portsmouth Evening Star* newspaper. The next year, he was thrilled to be promoted to sportswriter—and to be paid fifty cents per article. At seventeen, he joined the staff of the *Washington Daily News* in Washington, D.C.

During World War II (1939–1945), Taylor served in the U.S. Merchant Marines. Later, he joined the U.S. Naval Reserve. His duties at sea led him to posts in both the Atlantic and Pacific oceans. His seafaring experiences would provide the background for many of his later books.

Taylor married Gweneth Goodwin in 1946, and they had three children—Mark, Wendy, and Michael. In the 1950s, the family moved to California. There Taylor worked as a screenwriter for several Hollywood movie studios. His kids were curious about the movie business, and that gave

> *"Every story I have written is about real people and stems from real-life events. They include kids who have figured out things for themselves because kids like that really exist."*

BEFORE TED BECAME AN ADULT, SOME OF HIS EARLY JOBS INCLUDED PLUCKING CHICKENS, FISHING FOR CRABS, DELIVERING FALSE TEETH, AND ASSISTING BOXERS.

A Selected Bibliography of Taylor's Work

Billy the Kid: A Novel (2005)

Ice Drift (2004)

The Boy Who Could Fly without a Motor (2002)

A Rogue Wave and Other Red-Blooded Sea Stories (1996)

The Bomb (1995)

Timothy of the Cay (1993)

Tuck Triumphant (1991)

The Weirdo (1991)

Sniper (1989)

Walking up a Rainbow (1986)

The Trouble with Tuck (1981)

The Odyssey of Ben O'Neal (1977)

A Shepherd Watches, A Shepherd Sings (with Louis Irigaray, 1977)

Battle in the Arctic Seas: The Story of Convoy PQ 17 (1976)

Teetoncey and Ben O'Neal (1975)

Teetoncey (1974)

People Who Make Movies (1967)

The Cay (1969)

Taylor's Major Literary Award

1996 Scott O'Dell Award
   The Bomb

Taylor the idea for his first children's book, *People Who Make Movies*, published in 1967.

Taylor's next book was *The Cay*. It's about a white boy who learns to overcome his prejudice when he and a black man are shipwrecked together on an island. *The Cay* was published in 1969, and Taylor retired from the movie industry the next year to be a full-time writer.

Taylor offers up more sea adventures in his Cape Hatteras trilogy—*Teetoncey*, *Teetoncey and Ben O'Neal*, and *The Odyssey of Ben O'Neal*. All three books take place off the coast of North Carolina. They follow the exploits of a shipwrecked English girl and a fatherless boy in the 1800s.

"I believe that a writer should constantly feed his fires by being on the go, doing different things, seeking new experiences."

Taylor went on to write more than fifty books, some for adults but most for young people. His juvenile books are both fiction and nonfiction. Many of Taylor's nonfiction books are about war. In his fiction stories, his young characters often overcome horrendous situations to emerge as strong, self-reliant individuals.

Taylor and his second wife, Flora, live in Laguna Beach, California.

❧

WHERE TO FIND OUT MORE ABOUT THEODORE TAYLOR

BOOKS

Drew, Bernard A. *The One Hundred Most Popular Young Adult Authors.* Englewood, Colo.: Libraries Unlimited, 1996.

Silvey, Anita, ed. *The Essential Guide to Children's Books and Their Creators.* Boston: Houghton Mifflin Company, 2002.

WEB SITES

HARCOURT TRADE PUBLISHERS
http://www.harcourtbooks.com/authorinterviews/bookinterview_taylor.asp
For a transcript of an interview with Taylor

THEODORE TAYLOR HOME PAGE
http://www.theodoretaylor.com/index.htm
For a biography, list of books, and information about works in progress

———

TAYLOR USUALLY REWRITES A BOOK FOUR OR FIVE TIMES BEFORE HE CONSIDERS IT FINISHED.

J. R. R. Tolkien

Born: January 3, 1892
Died: September 2, 1973

J. R. R. Tolkien created his own world filled with strange characters. His books tell the story of a fantasy world called Middle-earth where readers meet hobbits, elves, dwarfs, and orcs. Tolkien is best known as the author of *The Hobbit; or, There and Back Again* and The Lord of the Rings trilogy. His books were written decades ago yet remain popular with young readers.

John Ronald Reuel (J. R. R.) Tolkien was born on January 3, 1892, in Bloemfontein, South Africa, where his father was a bank manager. When Ronald was three, his mother took him and his brother back to England. His father stayed in South Africa, planning to join his family later. Ronald's father died in 1896, however, before he could move back to England. Ronald's mother was left to raise Ronald and his brother by herself.

IN 2002, A FIRST EDITION OF *THE HOBBIT* SOLD FOR MORE THAN $60,000. IT WAS THE HIGHEST PRICE EVER PAID FOR A TOLKIEN BOOK.

Ronald's mother introduced him to reading, writing, and her love of words. She also encouraged her sons to have a strong faith in the Catholic Church.

When Ronald was about twelve years old, his mother died of diabetes. Before her death, she arranged for Father Francis Xavier Morgan, a Catholic priest, to be her children's guardian. Father Morgan raised the boys, taught them a great deal, and helped pay for their education.

A Selected Bibliography of Tolkien's Work
Roverandom (1998)
The Silmarillion (with Christopher Tolkien, 1977)
The Father Christmas Letters (1976)
The Return of the King (1955)
The Fellowship of the Ring (1954)
The Two Towers (1954)
Farmer Giles of Ham (1949)
The Hobbit; or, There and Back Again (1937)

"If you really want to know what Middle-earth is based on, it's my wonder and delight in the earth as it is, particularly the natural earth."

As a student, Ronald loved the study of languages. Like many students at the time, he learned Latin and Greek. He also taught himself to speak and write several other languages.

> *"I had the habit while my children were still young of inventing and telling orally, sometimes of writing down, 'children's stories' for their private amusement. The* Hobbit *was intended to be one of them."*

Tolkien was a student at Oxford University when he began writing. After serving in the army in World War I (1914–1918), he took a job working with the *Oxford English Dictionary* for about two years. He then went on to become a professor of English at Oxford University.

Tolkien began writing *The Hobbit; or, There and Back Again* while teaching at Oxford. It was published in 1937 and was a great success. Later that same year, he began writing another book as a sequel to *The Hobbit.*

It took Tolkien more than eleven years to finish The Lord of the Rings trilogy. He was busy with his teaching schedule, but he rewrote parts of the story many times. The first two parts of the trilogy, *The Fellowship of the Ring* and *The Two Towers,* were published in 1954. The third part, *The Return of the King,* was not released until late 1955. The Lord of the Rings trilogy was a financial success for Tolkien and was translated into many languages.

THE THREE VOLUMES OF THE THE LORD OF THE RINGS HAVE BEEN ADAPTED INTO MOTION PICTURES. THE FIRST FILM, *THE FELLOWSHIP OF THE RING,* WAS RELEASED IN 2001.

Tolkien's books continue to be popular today. His stories have been adapted for television and motion pictures.

J. R. R. Tolkien died on September 2, 1973, in England. He was eighty-one years old.

&

WHERE TO FIND OUT MORE ABOUT J. R. R. TOLKIEN

BOOKS

Becker, Alida, ed. *The Tolkien Scrapbook.*
Philadelphia: Running Press, 1978.

Hammond, Wayne G., and Christina Scull, eds.
J. R. R. Tolkien: Artist and Illustrator.
Boston: Houghton Mifflin, 2000.

Niemark, Anne E., and Brad Weinman, ill.
Myth Maker: J. R. R. Tolkien.
New York: Harcourt, 1996.

WEB SITES

TOLKIEN
http://www.tolkien.co.uk/frame.asp
To read information about Tolkien and his books

THE TOLKIEN SOCIETY
http://www.tolkiensociety.org/index.html
An extensive site dedicated to J. R. R. Tolkien

AT THE TIME OF HIS DEATH, TOLKIEN WAS WORKING ON HIS BOOK
THE SILMARILLION. HIS SON CHRISTOPHER COMPLETED THE BOOK
AND PUBLISHED IT FOUR YEARS LATER.

P. L. Travers

Born: August 9, 1899
Died: April 23, 1996

Who wouldn't want to be raised by Mary Poppins? She is magical and marvelous, stern and tender, secretive and proud, and more than a little bit vain. To millions of children around the world, Mary Poppins is the ultimate British nanny.

Mary Poppins is the creation of Pamela Lyndon Travers, who was born Helen Lyndon Goff in Queensland, Australia, on August 9, 1899. As a child, Helen loved fairy tales and magic. "I shall never know," Travers once wrote, "which good lady it was who, at my own christening, gave me the everlasting gift, spotless amid all spotted joys, of love for the fairy tale."

Whether it was because of a fairy godmother or her own story-telling parents, Helen grew up reading and writing poems and stories. In

A STATUE OF MARY POPPINS STANDS IN NEW YORK CITY'S
CENTRAL PARK. P. L. TRAVERS POSED FOR IT IN 1963.

her grown-up years, Travers would say that she couldn't remember a time when she didn't write. Writing—mostly fairy tales about magical beings—came as naturally to her as breathing.

Even more than writing, Helen loved theater. She loved everything about the

> "Mary Poppins's chief characteristic, apart from her tremendous vanity, is that she never explains. I often wonder why people write and ask me to explain this and that. I'll write back and say that Mary Poppins didn't explain, so neither can I or neither will I."

stage—writing plays, acting in plays, and producing plays. She was always involved in her school's theatrical productions, and she performed in her first "real" play when she was only ten.

By then, Helen and her mother and two younger sisters were living on a sugar plantation in New South Wales with her great-aunt Sass. Her father had died when she was only seven—the first great sorrow of her life. But Aunt Sass stepped in to take care of the family. She became part of the inspiration for Mary Poppins.

As she grew older, Helen (who took the stage name Pamela Lyndon Travers) continued acting and writing. She worked with traveling Shakespearean companies when she was a teenager and had her first poems published when she was just sixteen.

———

TRAVERS GUARDED HER PRIVACY WITH GREAT CARE. AFTER WRITING *MARY POPPINS,* SHE SIGNED HER BOOKS WITH HER INITIALS ONLY. USING HER INITIALS SEEMED ONE WAY TO HIDE HERSELF.

Mary Poppins

P. L. Travers

A Selected Bibliography of Travers's Work
Friend Monkey (1971)
I Go by Sea, I Go by Land (1964)
Mary Poppins in the Park (1952)
Mary Poppins Opens the Door (1943)
Aunt Sass (1941)
Mary Poppins Comes Back (1935)
Mary Poppins (1934)

But Travers wanted more. Carefully saving the money she earned from acting, she soon had enough to travel to Great Britain. This was where her mother and father came from. To Travers, it felt like home.

Travers was talented and lucky, and she soon found work as a journalist. She also published poems in the *Irish Statesman,* a famous literary magazine, and became friends with some of the best writers of the time.

Travers earned her own fame when she published *Mary Poppins* in 1934. She wrote the book in an old thatched house in the English countryside, while she was recovering from a long illness. Friends insisted that she

send the story to a publisher—
and the rest is history.

Travers wrote a number
of sequels about Mary Poppins
and the Banks children she
cares for so primly, magically,
and lovingly. The Mary Poppins

"I think the idea of Mary Poppins has been blowing in and out of me, like a curtain at a window, all my life. My sister assures me that I told her stories of Mary Poppins when we were very small children."

titles are still beloved by millions of children all around the world. P. L.
Travers died in London, England, on April 23, 1996.

WHERE TO FIND OUT MORE ABOUT P. L. TRAVERS

BOOKS

Demers, Patricia. *P. L. Travers.* New York: Twayne Publications, 1991.

Draper, Ellen Dooling, and Jenny Koralek, eds. *A Lively Oracle: A Centennial Celebration of P. L. Travers, Creator of Mary Poppins.* Burdett, N.Y.: Larson Publications, 1999.

Lawson, Valerie. *Out of the Sky She Came.* London: Hodder Headline Group, 1999.

WEB SITES

AMERICAN SOCIETY OF AUTHORS AND WRITERS
http://amsaw.org/amsaw-ithappenedinhistory-080904-travers.html
For biographical information about the author

FANTASTIC FICTION
http://www.fantasticfiction.co.uk/authors/P_L_Travers.htm
For information about Travers's writing

ONE OF TRAVERS'S FAVORITE CHILDHOOD GAMES INVOLVED MAKING A NEST IN THE FIELD OF WEEDS ALONGSIDE HER HOUSE AND PRETENDING SHE WAS A BIRD LAYING EGGS. HER MOTHER PLAYED RIGHT ALONG WITH HER!

Yoshiko Uchida

Born: November 24, 1921
Died: June 21, 1992

As a Japanese American, Yoshiko Uchida brought her cultural heritage to life in more than thirty books for children and young adults. While some of her books are Japanese folktales, others reveal the hardships of Japanese American children in the United States.

Yoshiko Uchida was born in Alameda, California, in 1921. Both her parents were immigrants from Japan. The family eventually moved to the city of Berkeley, California, and Yoshiko and her older sister, Keiko, spent their childhood there.

Yoshiko's mother often wrote Japanese poetry, and Yoshiko herself began writing stories at an early age. When she was ten, she wrote "Willy the Squirrel" and other stories on brown wrapping paper. At twelve, she wrote and illustrated a seven-chapter book called "Sally Jane Waters."

After graduating from University High School in Oakland, California, she enrolled in the University of California at Berkeley. In 1942, she earned a bachelor's degree with honors, but she didn't get to attend her

---

WHILE SHE WAS AT THE TOPAZ RELOCATION CAMP,
UCHIDA TAUGHT AT AN ELEMENTARY SCHOOL THERE.

own graduation ceremony. Just two weeks before graduation, her life was changed forever.

During World War II (1939–1945), Japanese Americans were considered a threat to national security and were imprisoned in camps. The entire Uchida family was sent to live at Tanforan Racetrack in San Bruno, California. There, in crowded and cramped conditions, people were forced to stay in horse stables. Then the family was transferred to the Topaz Relocation Camp in the desert near Delta, Utah.

In 1943, Uchida obtained permission to leave Topaz and attend Smith College in Northampton, Massachusetts. There she earned a master's

A Selected Bibliography of Uchida's Work

The Wise Old Woman (1994)
The Magic Purse (1993)
The Invisible Thread: An Autobiography (1991)
The Happiest Ending (1985)
The Best Bad Thing (1983)
Desert Exile: The Uprooting of a Japanese-American Family (1982)
A Jar of Dreams (1981)
Samurai of Gold Hill (1972)
Journey to Topaz (1971)
Sumi and the Goat and the Tokyo Express (1969)
Takao and Grandfather's Sword (1958)
The Magic Listening Cap (1955)
The Dancing Kettle and Other Japanese Folk Tales (1949)

> *"I write to celebrate our common humanity, for the basic elements of humanity are present in all our strivings."*

degree in education in 1944. After teaching for a year, she decided to work as a secretary. That gave her more time for her writing, and she began sending short stories to magazines. She mostly received rejections, but editors often attached encouraging notes. In 1949, she published her first book—*The Dancing Kettle and Other Japanese Folk Tales.*

In 1952, Uchida received a fellowship from the Ford Foundation, which allowed her to study in a foreign country. She spent that time in Japan, collecting more folktales and learning about Japanese arts and crafts. During her visit, Uchida also gained a greater awareness of her own identity as

> *"Through my books I hope to give young Asian Americans a sense of their past and to reinforce their self-esteem and self-knowledge."*

a Japanese American, and she came to admire the culture that had formed her parents' outlook.

From the mid-1950s through the 1960s, Uchida cared for her aging parents back in Oakland. During that time, she wrote children's books that revealed many aspects of Japanese life and customs. By 1971, both of Uchida's parents had died. She moved to Berkeley, where she lived for the rest of her life.

YOSHIKO UCHIDA COMPLETED HIGH SCHOOL IN ONLY TWO AND A HALF YEARS.

That same year, Uchida's book *Journey to Topaz* was published. It tells the tale of a Japanese American family's relocation to a wartime camp. *Desert Exile* is an even more personal story. It recounts the Uchida family's experiences during the war. Subsequent books include more Japanese folktales, as well as other stories about the struggles of Japanese American children.

Uchida died in Berkeley at the age of seventy.

❧

WHERE TO FIND OUT MORE ABOUT YOSHIKO UCHIDA

BOOKS

Marvis, Barbara J. *Contemporary American Success Stories: Famous People of Asian Ancestry.* Bear, Del.: Mitchell Lane Publishers, 1993.

McElmeel, Sharron L. *100 Most Popular Children's Authors: Biographical Sketches and Bibliographies.* Englewood, Colo.: Libraries Unlimited, 1999.

Uchida, Yoshiko. *Invisible Thread: A Memoir by Yoshiko Uchida.* Hampstead, Tex.: Sagebrush, 1999.

WEB SITES

PENGUIN GROUP
http://us.penguingroup.com/nf/Author/AuthorPage/0,,0_1000040395,00.html
To read a short biography about Yoshiko Uchida

YOSHIKO UCHIDA
*http://64.172.206.2/Internet/StudentLife/Projects/AuthorWebPages04/
Katherine-Gard/homepage.htm*
For a biography, book listings, awards, and links

———

MORE THAN 100,000 JAPANESE AMERICANS WERE RELOCATED TO CAMPS DURING WORLD WAR II. MOST OF THEM WERE AMERICAN CITIZENS.

Chris Van Allsburg

Born: June 18, 1949

Chris Van Allsburg is best known for the mysterious feelings in the stories he writes and in the beautiful illustrations he creates for them. Sometimes Van Allsburg makes bizarre events look believable. In *Jumanji,* a herd of rhinoceroses charges into a family's living room and pythons appear above the fireplace, but Van Allsburg draws the scene so it looks almost normal. On the other hand, the artist knows how to make even the most ordinary scene look odd—as if something strange is

going on. "Think of it this way," Van Allsburg says. "The style I use allows me to make a drawing that has a little mystery to it, even if the actual things I am drawing are not strange or mysterious."

This quality has helped make Van Allsburg one of the best-known children's illustrators. He has twice won the Caldecott Medal, one of the highest awards for picture books. *Jumanji* was made into a

---

VAN ALLSBURG SAYS KIDS AREN'T ON HIS MIND WHEN HE WRITES HIS BOOKS. "WHEN
I SET OUT TO TELL A STORY, I'M JUST TRYING TO INTEREST MYSELF," HE EXPLAINS.

movie, as was *The Polar Express*, one of the most popular books in any library.

Chris Van Allsburg was born on June 18, 1949, in Grand Rapids, Michigan. He says he did "normal kid things," while he was growing up—catching tadpoles, playing baseball, and building model planes and trucks. He attended the University of Michigan where two important things happened to him: He met Lisa Morrison, the woman he would marry, while teaching her how to use a power saw in an art class. And he discovered that he wanted to be an artist.

After college, Van Allsburg continued to study art at the Rhode Island School of Design

A Selected Bibliography of Van Allsburg's Work

Probuditi! (2006)
Zathura: Brothers Together (2005)
Gift of Christmas (2004)
Zathura: A Space Adventure (2002)
The Veil of Snows (Illustrations only, 1997)
A City in Winter (Illustrations only, 1996)
Just a Dream (1990)
The Alphabet Theatre Proudly Presents the Z Was Zapped: A Play in Twenty-Six Acts (1987)
The Stranger (1986)
The Polar Express (1985)
The Mysteries of Harris Burdick (1984)
The Wreck of the Zephyr (1983)
Ben's Dream: Story and Pictures (1982)
Jumanji (1981)
The Garden of Abdul Gasazi (1979)

Van Allsburg's Major Literary Awards

1986 Boston Globe-Horn Book Picture Book Honor Book
1986 Caldecott Medal
    The Polar Express

1985 Boston Globe-Horn Book Picture Book Honor Book
    The Mysteries of Harris Burdick

1982 Caldecott Medal
1981 Boston Globe-Horn Book Picture Book Honor Book
    Jumanji

1980 Boston Globe-Horn Book Picture Book Award
1980 Caldecott Honor Book
    The Garden of Abdul Gasazi

(where he was also a teacher for more than ten years). He was mostly interested in sculpture and exhibited his work at important museums and galleries.

> *"The first book I remember reading [was about] Dick, Jane, and Spot. Actually, the lives of this trio were not all that interesting. A young reader's reward for struggling through those syllables at the bottom of the page was to discover that Spot got a bath. Not exactly an exciting revelation."*

Van Allsburg's wife persuaded him to try his hand at a children's book. His first story, *The Garden of Abdul Gasazi,* was published in 1979. It is about a dog that escapes into a magician's garden and (maybe) gets turned into a duck. The book was a success.

Van Allsburg's second book, *Jumanji,* was an even greater success, winning him his first Caldecott Medal. The story is about a board game that causes magical problems in the home of two bored children. In 1983 came *The Wreck of the Zephyr,* Van Allsburg's first book in color. And in 1985, Van Allsburg published *The Polar Express,* his very popular Christmas fable.

Van Allsburg has written close to twenty books for children, including *The Alphabet Theatre Proudly Presents the Z Was Zapped: A Play in Twenty-Six Acts.* Some of his books include interesting experiments. For instance, *The Mysteries of Harris Burdick* consists of a set of strange illustrations. The

_____

IN A SPECIAL ANNIVERSARY EDITION OF *THE POLAR EXPRESS,* VAN ALLSBURG ADDED AN INTRODUCTION EXPLAINING THAT HE STOLE THE STORY FROM A BEGGAR CHILD ONE COLD NIGHT. SOME PEOPLE DIDN'T REALIZE VAN ALLSBURG WAS JOKING.

book says that the story has been lost and readers will have to make up their own.

Van Allsburg lives and works in an old house in Providence, Rhode Island. He and his wife have two daughters.

"I create a story by posing questions to myself. I call it the 'what if' and 'what then' approach. For example, for my book Jumanji, *I started out by thinking 'What if two bored children discovered a board game? What if the board game came to life? What then?' "*

WHERE TO FIND OUT MORE ABOUT CHRIS VAN ALLSBURG

BOOKS

Kovacs, Deborah, and James Preller. *Meet the Authors and Illustrators: 60 Creators of Favorite Children's Books Talk about Their Work.* Vol. 1. New York: Scholastic, 1991.

Palumbo, Tom. *Integrating the Literature of Chris Van Allsburg in the Classroom.* New York: McGraw-Hill Children's Publishing, 1996.

WEB SITES

ASK THE AUTHOR
http://www.eduplace.com/author/vanallsburg/
To read an interview with Chris Van Allsburg

CHRIS VAN ALLSBURG HOME PAGE
http://www.chrisvanallsburg.com/home.html
To read biographical information, news, a list of works, and a timeline

IN 1997, THE U.S. POSTAL SERVICE ISSUED A STAMP DESIGNED BY VAN ALLSBURG. THE THIRTY-TWO-CENT "HELPING CHILDREN LEARN" STAMP SHOWS A FATHER AND DAUGHTER READING TOGETHER.

Wendelin Van Draanen

Born: January 6

Wendelin Van Draanen is best known for her Sammy Keyes mystery series. The series' heroine, Samantha, is a spunky tomboy who prefers to be called Sammy. For young readers, Sammy is a realistic, believable character, and it's easy to see why. Van Draanen knows how a tomboy thinks and feels because she used to be a tomboy herself.

Wendelin Van Draanen was born in Chicago, Illinois. She often felt shy and out of place among other children, but she had a great time playing with her two brothers. "I did a lot of 'boy stuff,' " she recalls. They spied on neighbors, played ball, went camping and backpacking, and splashed in gutters full of rainwater.

VAN DRAANEN'S HOBBIES INCLUDE WHAT SHE CALLS THE
THREE R'S: "READING, RUNNING, AND ROCK 'N' ROLL."

One of her fond childhood memories was story time at night. With the kids snuggled around him, her father read from a book of children's stories. Wendelin learned to read at an early age, and she especially enjoyed mysteries such as the Nancy Drew, Hardy Boys, and Encyclopedia Brown series.

> *"It's my goal to get kids through those awkward years and onto adulthood safely. The choices they make . . . now will affect them their entire lives."*

Both of Wendelin's parents were chemists, and she was drawn to science, too. She still remembers how exciting it was when she learned computer programming, and she ultimately decided to pursue a career in computer science. While she was in college, a fire destroyed the family business. Van Draanen went home to help her parents out, and while she was there, she found herself wracked with feelings of anger and stress. To relieve the pressure, she wrote about the disastrous incident. She found writing to be soothing—and enjoyable.

After college, Van Draanen taught computer science to high school students. Meanwhile, she began writing novels for adults. After ten years, she had written ten novels, but none of them were accepted for publication. Then she decided to try writing with the voice of a twelve-year-old. This time, she wrote about the mischief, miseries, and joys

---

VAN DRAANEN'S BOOKS HAVE BEEN PUBLISHED IN SEVEN FOREIGN LANGUAGES.

A Selected Bibliography of Van Draanen's Work

Runaway (2006)

Enemy Spy (2005)

Meet the Gecko (2005)

Sammy Keyes and the Dead Giveaway (2005)

Attack of the Tagger (2004)

Sammy Keyes and the Psycho Kitty Queen (2004)

Secret Identity (2004)

Sammy Keyes and the Art of Deception (2003)

Swear to Howdy (2003)

Sammy Keyes and the Search for Snake Eyes (2002)

Flipped (2001)

Sammy Keyes and the Hollywood Mummy (2001)

Sammy Keyes and the Curse of the Moustache Mary (2000)

Sammy Keyes and the Runaway Elf (1999)

Sammy Keyes and the Sisters of Mercy (1999)

Sammy Keyes and the Hotel Thief (1998)

Sammy Keyes and the Skeleton Man (1998)

How I Survived Being a Girl (1997)

she experienced growing up with her two brothers. *How I Survived Being a Girl*—Van Draanen's first published book—came out in 1997.

Van Draanen found that she wrote best when she used a twelve-year-old's point of view. In 1998, she launched the Sammy Keyes series with *Sammy Keyes and the Hotel Thief*. The next year, Van Draanen quit teaching to be a full-time writer.

Year after year, more Sammy Keyes books appeared. They all feature Sammy, the twelve-year-old tomboy who has a particular talent for solving mysteries. Much more goes on in these stories, though. As each mystery unfolds, the young characters do a lot of growing

> "*The best part of being a writer is the feeling it gives me that anything is possible.*"

up and discover their own strengths. Van Draanen is especially fond of Sammy. As she describes it, "Sammy's the friend I wish I'd had growing up."

In 2004, Van Draanen launched her Shredderman series with *Secret Identity*. These stories star Nolan Byrd, a slightly nerdy math whiz who fights for truth and justice as the superhero Shredderman. Like Sammy Keyes, Nolan finds the strength to do the right thing in difficult circumstances.

Van Draanen lives along the central California coast with her husband and two sons.

ॐ

WHERE TO FIND OUT MORE ABOUT WENDELIN VAN DRAANEN

WEB SITES
CHILDRENSLIT.COM
http://www.childrenslit.com/f_vandraanen.html
For a short biography of the author and reviews of her works

GIRLSTART.COM
http://www.girlstart.com/wendelin.asp
For an interview with Wendelin Van Draanen and links to other Web sites

KIDSREADS.COM
http://www.kidsreads.com/series/series-keyes-author.asp
To read a biography of Wendelin Van Draanen

———

VAN DRAANEN'S FAVORITE THINGS TO EAT ARE DARK CHOCOLATE AND SPICY MEXICAN FOODS.

Judith Viorst

Born: February 2, 1931

For more than thirty years, Judith Viorst has been reaching out to people of all ages through her writing. She has written everything from children's fiction and nonfiction to adult poetry and self-help books. Her best-loved books, though, are the ones she wrote about her own family. Young readers appreciate Viorst's honesty. She creates characters—kids and adults alike—who are not perfect and very human. Her stories help readers laugh at the problems that go along with being a kid.

Judith Viorst was born on February 2, 1931, in Newark, New Jersey. Even at an early age, Judith knew that she wanted to be a writer. One of the first things she ever wrote was a poem about her parents. As she grew older, Judith continued writing poetry and stories about her

---

VIORST'S PICTURE BOOKS TAKE SEVERAL MONTHS TO WRITE.
HER CHILDREN'S POETRY BOOKS TAKE ABOUT TWO YEARS.

life. She used her feelings as fuel for her writing. Although she tried to

get her work published, she was not successful.

After Viorst graduated from college, she moved to Greenwich Village in New York City. There she began her career in publishing, first as a secretary for a magazine. After she was married, Viorst moved to Washington, D.C. In Washington, she worked as an editor of science books. This gave Viorst her first chance to write for kids. From 1962 to 1967, she published four science books for teens.

> *"I like to take all my feelings and thoughts and put them down in different ways on paper."*

Viorst decided to try her hand at writing fiction when her three sons were growing up. Like other kids, Anthony, Nicholas, and Alexander had their share of day-to-day problems. Viorst wrote stories that she thought might help them—or at least might make them smile. The first book about her boys was *Sunday Morning: A Story,* published in 1968. *Sunday Morning* features two overactive youngsters named Anthony and Nick. Other books about Viorst's sons cover such topics as sibling rivalry, the death of a pet, and very bad days.

Viorst's most popular book for kids is *Alexander and the Terrible, Horrible, No Good, Very Bad Day.* The book was written in 1972, about Viorst's youngest son. Since it was published, the book has sold more than

---

JUDITH VIORST'S HUSBAND, MILTON, IS A POLITICAL WRITER WHO HAS COVERED THE MIDDLE EAST FOR MANY YEARS.

A Selected Bibliography of Viorst's Work

Just in Case (2005)

Super-Completely and Totally the Messiest (2000)

Alexander Who's Not (Do You Hear Me? I Mean It!) Going to Move (1995)

Sad Underwear and Other Complications: More Poems for Children and Their Parents (1995)

The Alphabet from Z to A: (With Much Confusion on the Way) (1993)

Earrings! (1990)

The Good-Bye Book (1988)

If I Were in Charge of the World and Other Worries: Poems for Children and Their Parents (1981)

Alexander, Who Used to Be Rich Last Sunday (1978)

Rosie and Michael (1974)

My Mama Says There Aren't Any Zombies, Ghosts, Vampires, Creatures, Demons, Monsters, Fiends, Goblins, or Things (1973)

Alexander and the Terrible, Horrible, No Good, Very Bad Day (1972)

The Tenth Good Thing about Barney (1971)

Try It Again, Sam; Safety When You Walk (1970)

I'll Fix Anthony (1969)

Sunday Morning: A Story (1968)

two million copies. Kids today still enjoy reading about Alexander's mishaps. In 1998, the book was made into a musical play, and Viorst wrote the lyrics. *Alexander* opened to rave reviews at the Kennedy Center in Washington, D.C., and later toured around the nation.

As her boys grew older, Viorst turned her attention to other kinds of writing. She has written books of poetry for kids and adults. She is well known to many adult readers for her humorous books about getting older. She has also written serious books for adults about marriage and grief. Viorst writes articles and columns for various magazines and newspapers, too.

Although her sons have all grown up and moved out of the house, Judith Viorst still writes for children from time to time. She has said that she hopes to keep writing children's books for as long as she lives.

> *"The writing of [children's books] gives me enormous joy and satisfaction."*

⚬⚭

WHERE TO FIND OUT MORE ABOUT JUDITH VIORST

BOOKS

McElmeel, Sharron L. *100 Most Popular Picture Book Authors and Illustrators: Biographical Sketches and Bibliographies.* Englewood, Colo.: Libraries Unlimited, 2000.

Mote, Dave. *Contemporary Popular Writers.* 1st ed. Detroit: St. James Press, 1996.

Silvey, Anita, ed. *The Essential Guide to Children's Books and Their Creators.* Boston: Houghton Mifflin Company, 2002.

Wheeler, Jill C. *Judith Viorst.* Edina, Minn.: Abdo & Daughters, 1997.

WEB SITES

FRIENDS OF THE OSU LIBRARY
http://www.library.okstate.edu/friends/cobb/viorst.htm
For an interview with and further information about Viorst

KENNEDY CENTER
http://kennedy-center.org/programs/family/alexander/author.html
To read a short biography of and an interview with Viorst

DRAMATIC PUBLISHING
http://www.dramaticpublishing.com/viorst.html
To read an autobiographical sketch by Viorst

———

JUDITH VIORST'S CHILDREN'S BOOKS HAVE BEEN TRANSLATED INTO MANY LANGUAGES, INCLUDING DUTCH, FRENCH, GERMAN, JAPANESE, AND SPANISH.

Cynthia Voigt

Born: February 25, 1942

C ynthia Voigt read a lot as a child. She liked reading series books such as Nancy Drew mysteries and Cherry Ames. Most of the books she enjoyed were given to her by her parents. When she found a copy of the children's classic *The Secret Garden* by Frances Hodgson Burnett at her grandmother's house, she not only loved the story, but was thrilled by the feeling of discovering a book all by herself. This thrill of discovery would carry over to her work as a teacher and a children's book author.

Cynthia Irving was born on February 25, 1942, in Boston, Massachusetts. Her mother's name was Elise Keeney, and her father, a corporate executive, was Frederick C. Irving. Young Cynthia was the second of four children. The family moved to Connecticut when she was in elementary school, and Cynthia had a fairly happy childhood.

ON TRIPS TO THE LIBRARY TO FIND BOOKS FOR HER FIFTH-GRADE STUDENTS, VOIGT WOULD SOMETIMES CHECK OUT AS MANY AS THIRTY BOOKS IN ONE DAY.

By the time she entered high school, Cynthia was aiming for a career as a writer. She loved reading, and she got a thrill out of making up her own stories. After graduating from Smith College in Massachusetts, she went to St. Michael's College in Santa Fe, New Mexico, for her graduate work.

She was working at an advertising agency in New York City when she and Walter Voight got married in 1964. They soon moved to Sante Fe. In college, Cynthia Voigt had vowed never to be a teacher.

"I enjoy almost everything I do, perhaps because when I don't enjoy something, I don't do it."

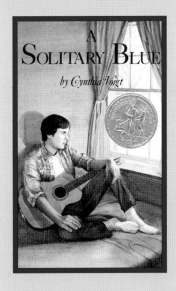

A Selected Bibliography of Voigt's Work

Angus and Sadie (2005)
It's Not Easy Being Bad (2000)
Elske (1999)
Bad Girls (1996)
The Wings of a Falcon (1993)
Orfe (1992)
David and Jonathan (1991)
Glass Mountain: A Novel (1991)
Seventeen against the Dealer (1989)
Sons from Afar (1987)
Come a Stranger (1986)
Izzy, Willy-Nilly (1986)
Jackaroo (1985)
The Runner (1985)
Building Blocks (1984)
The Callender Papers (1983)
A Solitary Blue (1983)
Dicey's Song (1982)
Homecoming (1981)

Voigt's Major Literary Awards

1984 Boston Globe–Horn Book Fiction Honor Book
1984 Newbery Honor Book
   A Solitary Blue

1983 Boston Globe–Horn Book Fiction Honor Book
1983 Newbery Medal
   Dicey's Song

> "I always wanted to be a writer, always from the age of twelve. Even earlier than that I was a reader. I love a good story, and I love to meet interesting characters, and I like thinking."

But in Santa Fe, she began teaching fourth and fifth grade, and she quickly discovered that she loved teaching.

Voigt's plans to become a writer were put on hold while she raised her children. After her divorce in 1972, she moved to Maryland, got a teaching job, and decided to try her hand at writing for children. Establishing a regular routine of writing for a minimum of one hour a day, Voigt began working on her first book, *Homecoming.*

After she remarried in 1974, Voigt decided to teach only part time, so she could dedicate more time to her writing. *Homecoming,* which introduced the character of Dicey Tillerman, was published in 1981.

Cynthia Voigt's second book about the Tillermans, *Dicey's Song,* won the 1983 Newbery Medal and established her as an important voice in children's literature. *Dicey's Song* tells of how thirteen-year-old Dicey Tillerman takes care of her younger brothers and sisters after their emotionally disturbed mother abandons them. So far, Voigt has written seven books about the Tillermans.

IN ADDITION TO WORKING IN ADVERTISING AND AS A TEACHER, VOIGT HAS BEEN A CHILD-CARE PROVIDER, A SECRETARY, AND A WAITRESS.

Voigt is constantly jotting down story ideas and lists of characters. Sometimes her ideas bounce around in her mind for more than a year before she starts turning them into a book.

In her leisure time, Voigt enjoys reading, playing tennis, seeing movies, and spending time at the beach with her children. Her many fans enjoy spending their free time reading the books of Cynthia Voigt.

❧

WHERE TO FIND OUT MORE ABOUT CYNTHIA VOIGT

BOOKS

Drew, Bernard A. *The 100 Most Popular Young Adult Authors: Biographical Sketches and Bibliographies.* Englewood, Colo.: Libraries Unlimited, 1996.

Jordan, Shirley Marie, ed. *Broken Silences: Interviews with Black and White Women Writers.* Piscataway, N.J.: Rutgers University Press, 1993.

Kovacs, Deborah, and James Preller. *Meet the Authors and Illustrators: 60 Creators of Favorite Children's Books Talk about Their Work.* Vol. 2. New York: Scholastic, 1993.

McElmeel, Sharron L. *100 Most Popular Children's Authors: Biographical Sketches and Bibliographies.* Englewood, Colo.: Libraries Unlimited, 1999.

WEB SITES

CYNTHIA VOIGT
http://gyabooks.tripod.com/voigt.html
To read short synopses of Voigt's books

EDUCATIONAL PAPERBACK ASSOCIATION
http://edupaperback.org/showauth.cfm?authid=109
For biographical information about Voigt

———

CYNTHIA VOIGT WON THE NEWBERY MEDAL FOR *DICEY'S SONG,* THE CALIFORNIA YOUNG READER'S AWARD FOR *IZZY, WILLY-NILLY,* AND THE EDGAR ALLAN POE AWARD FOR *THE CALLENDER PAPERS.*

Bernard Waber

Born: September 27, 1924

Bernard Waber discovered his love for children's books after his own children were born. He loved to read books to them. They often wondered why he was always reading children's books instead of books for adults. One day, he decided that he could write and illustrate books for children. Since then, Waber has created more than thirty books for children. His best-known books include *Lyle, Lyle, Crocodile; The House on East 88th Street; Nobody Is Perfick;* and *Ira Sleeps Over.*

Waber was born on September 27, 1924, in Philadelphia, Pennsylvania. He grew up during the Great Depression, and his family did not have much money. Bernard and his family moved many times so

---

LYLE, LYLE, CROCODILE HAS BEEN MADE INTO A MUSICAL PLAY
AND AN ANIMATED TELEVISION SPECIAL.

his father could find work. Each time his family moved, Bernard hoped there would be a library and a movie theater near their new house.

> *"Like food and drink, I considered the library and movies life-giving staples, and could not conceive of survival without them. The library, with its great store of un-required reading, was a banquet to which I brought a ravenous appetite."*

Bernard loved books and reading. He went to the library as often as he could. He also loved going to the movies. He spent almost every Saturday at the movie theater. When he was eight years old, he got a job as an usher at a movie theater. This job enabled him to watch the last ten or fifteen minutes of each movie, and he used his imagination to make up stories for the beginning and the middle of the movie.

Bernard was the youngest child in his family, and he often copied what his older brother was doing. "The youngest of four children, I was accustomed to all manner of hand-me-downs from an older brother," Waber remembers. "Luckily, my brother also handed down his great interest in drawing." Bernard spent hours drawing pictures that he saw in magazines.

In 1942, Waber joined the army. After that, he decided to study painting and drawing. He enrolled in an art school in Philadelphia.

SINCE WABER CREATED LYLE THE CROCODILE IN HIS BOOKS, HE HAS FOUND MANY DIFFERENT CROCODILE DECORATIONS FOR HIS HOME.

Lyle, Lyle, Crocodile
by BERNARD WABER

A Selected Bibliography of Waber's Work

Betty's Day Off (2005)

Evie and Margie (2003)

Fast Food! Gulp! Gulp! (2001)

The Mouse That Snored (2000)

Gina (1995)

Nobody Is Perfick (1991)

Ira Says Goodbye (1988)

Bernard (1982)

Dear Hildegarde (1980)

Ira Sleeps Over (1972)

A Firefly Named Torchy (1970)

An Anteater Named Arthur (1967)

Lyle, Lyle, Crocodile (1965)

Just Like Abraham Lincoln (1964)

The House on East 88th Street (1962)

Lorenzo (1961)

Waber married Ethel Bernstein in 1952 and moved to New York City. He worked as an illustrator and designer for a magazine publishing company. He loved this job because he got to work with many other talented artists. He went on to work for several magazines during his career.

In addition to his magazine work, Waber became interested

> *"Strangely, writing seems to come easier for me while I am in transit. I commute daily to Manhattan. As the train rattles onward, the rhythm of the wheels and the rocking motion somehow give my thoughts a fresh release."*

in creating a children's book. His friends and coworkers encouraged him. His first book, *Lorenzo,* was published in 1961. His books have won many awards and remain popular with children.

Bernard Waber continues to write and illustrate children's books. He also visits schools and libraries to talk about his books. He lives in Baldwin Harbor, New York.

⚬

WHERE TO FIND OUT MORE ABOUT BERNARD WABER

BOOKS

Kovacs, Deborah, and James Preller. *Meet the Authors and Illustrators: 60 Creators of Favorite Children's Books Talk about Their Work.* Vol. 1. New York: Scholastic, 1991.

McElmeel, Sharron L. *100 Most Popular Picture Book Authors and Illustrators: Biographical Sketches and Bibliographies.* Englewood, Colo.: Libraries Unlimited, 2000.

Silvey, Anita, ed. *The Essential Guide to Children's Books and Their Creators.* Boston: Houghton Mifflin Company, 2002.

WEB SITES

HOUGHTON MIFFLIN BOOKS
http://www.houghtonmifflinbooks.com/authors/waber/
For information about the author and his works

IRA SAYS GOODBYE
http://www.carolhurst.com/titles/irasaysgoodbye.html
For a review and relevant information
about Bernard Waber's book

———

WHEN HE WAS STARTING OUT AS AN ILLUSTRATOR, WABER WORKED AT THE DINING-ROOM TABLE IN HIS SMALL APARTMENT. HE MOVED TO A SEPARATE STUDIO LATER IN HIS CAREER.

Martin Waddell

Born: April 10, 1941

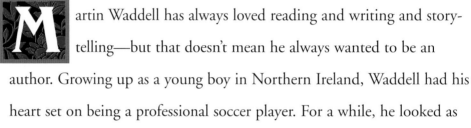

Martin Waddell has always loved reading and writing and story-telling—but that doesn't mean he always wanted to be an author. Growing up as a young boy in Northern Ireland, Waddell had his heart set on being a professional soccer player. For a while, he looked as if he would succeed!

Martin Waddell was born on April 10, 1941, in Belfast, Northern Ireland. This was in the middle of World War II (1939–1945), and German bombs were falling the night he was born. To keep their new baby safe, Martin's parents moved to the country town of Newcastle, in County Down, where his family had lived for almost 400 years. The Waddells moved back to Belfast after the war but always returned to Newcastle for holidays and summer

MARTIN WADDELL USUALLY SPENDS SEVERAL WEEKS EACH YEAR GIVING WRITING WORKSHOPS IN SCHOOLS IN NORTHERN IRELAND.

vacations. When his parents divorced when he was eleven, Martin and his mother moved back to Newcastle for good.

Martin wasn't particularly fond of school. He quit when he was just fifteen. He took a short-lived job at a newspaper and then moved to London when he was sixteen, hoping to win a place on a professional soccer team. Although Martin had been a fine goalie on his Newcastle team, he soon discovered that he didn't quite

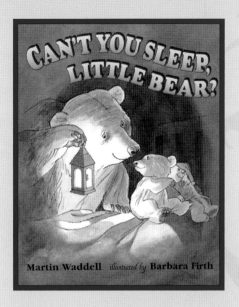

"My job as a writer is not to tell children what to think or do about a given situation, but to encourage them to think for themselves."

Waddell's Major Literary Award
2004 Hans Christian Andersen Medal for Authors

have what it took to be a professional athlete. That's when he turned to writing as a career. After several years—and a whole stack of rejected novels—he finally made a name for himself as a successful author of comic spy thrillers for adults.

Waddell earned enough money from his books to move back to Ireland, get married, and buy a house. But it wasn't until he published his first book for children in 1972, *In a Blue Velvet Dress,* that Waddell finally found his voice. He remembers, "My lyrical novels weren't even publishable. The thrillers were hopelessly padded to make the length, but *Blue Velvet* was full of fun and adventure and emotion. I had got it right, at last!"

> *"I was lucky. I grew up with books, so the transition from being a reader to being a writer was always possible. When I write books for the very small, I have this period in mind."*

He never looked back. Waddell has been writing steadily for almost forty years. By his own count, he's finished about 180 books!

Waddell has written children's books of all genres—mysteries and picture books, comedies and ghost stories, books about soccer players and baby bears and farmer ducks and accident-prone children. Many of his books, especially those written for very young children, were inspired by his own three sons, who are now grown up and living on their own.

IN 1972, WADDELL WAS NEARLY KILLED BY A TERRORIST BOMB IN A LOCAL CHURCH. HE WAS SO AFFECTED BY THE EVENT THAT HE WAS UNABLE TO WRITE FOR THE NEXT SIX YEARS.

Waddell takes even his most lighthearted books seriously, feeling that books for children need to be "quick, clear, emotionally strong, and verbally bright." He has won many awards, and his work has been made into radio and television programs. He and his wife still live in Newcastle, Northern Ireland—his first home, and his best home.

༨

WHERE TO FIND OUT MORE ABOUT MARTIN WADDELL

BOOKS

Holtze, Sally Holmes, ed. *Seventh Book of Junior Authors & Illustrators.* New York: H. W. Wilson Company, 1996.

Pendergast, Sara, and Tom Pendergast, eds. *St. James Guide to Children's Writers.* 5th ed. Detroit: St. James Press, 1999.

WEB SITES

THE ALAN REVIEW
http://scholar.lib.vt.edu/ejournals/ALAN/spring99/waddell.html
To read a message from Martin Waddell

O'BRIEN PRESS
http://www.obrien.ie/author.cfm?authorID=61
For a short biography and information about many of Waddell's books

WHEN WADDELL FIRST STARTED WRITING BOOKS FOR CHILDREN, HE USED THE NAME CATHERINE SEFTON, SO YOUNG READERS WOULDN'T CONFUSE HIM WITH THE MARTIN WADDELL WHO WROTE COMEDIES AND THRILLERS FOR ADULTS.

Gertrude Chandler Warner

Born: April 16, 1890
Died: August 30, 1979

As a young girl, Gertrude Chandler Warner lived near a railroad station. Her memories of watching the train cars were an important part of her writing as a children's author. Warner is best known as the creator and writer of many of the books in the Boxcar Children series. Along with the nineteen Boxcar Children books,

Warner also wrote fifteen other books for adults and children.

Gertrude Chandler Warner was born on April 16, 1890, in Putnam, Connecticut. She lived in Putnam her entire life. Gertrude

---

THE AMERICAN RED CROSS HONORED GERTRUDE CHANDLER WARNER FOR HER FIFTY YEARS OF SERVICE AS A VOLUNTEER WITH THE ORGANIZATION.

was often sick as a child, so she spent much of her time reading books and writing stories.

> *"As children, we received from our mother a ten-cent blank book to prevent the house from being littered with scraps of paper containing a 'good word' or a full sentence, or even a whole article."*

Her sister, Frances, shared her love of reading and writing. Their mother gave the girls notebooks so they could write their stories. Both girls also kept daily journals when they were growing up.

When Gertrude was nine years old, she wrote and illustrated her first book. The title of the book was "Golliwogg at the Zoo." She gave it to her grandfather as a Christmas present. Every year, Gertrude and her sister gave her grandparents a book they had created.

Because of her poor health, Gertrude was not able to finish high school. She and her sister wrote stories and essays that were published in local magazines. Her first published book, *The House of Delight*, came out in 1916. The book was about her experiences as a young girl playing with her dollhouse. In 1917, she went to work for the Red Cross as a writer and to help with publicity.

Warner was about twenty-eight years old when World War I (1914–1918) ended. It was a time when schools had a difficult time finding teachers. Even though she had not finished high school or

---

AS AN ADULT, WARNER USED THE SAME KIND OF NOTEBOOKS FOR HER RESEARCH AND NOTES THAT SHE HAD USED WHEN SHE WAS A YOUNG GIRL.

A Selected Bibliography of Warner's Work

Mystery behind the Wall (1973)

Mystery in the Sand (1971)

Bicycle Mystery (1970)

Snowbound Mystery (1968)

Houseboat Mystery (1967)

Caboose Mystery (1966)

Schoolhouse Mystery (1965)

The Lighthouse Mystery (1963)

The Woodshed Mystery (1962)

Blue Bay Mystery (1961)

Mystery Ranch (1958)

The Yellow House Mystery (1953)

Surprise Island (1949)

The Boxcar Children, Revised Edition (1942)

The Boxcar Children (1924)

The House of Delight (1916)

attended college, Warner was hired as a teacher. She taught first grade in Putnam for more than thirty years, retiring from teaching when she was sixty years old.

The first Boxcar Children book was published in 1924. Eighteen years later, Warner revised the book so it would be easier for children who struggled to read. She wanted to make her stories interesting to encourage children who had trouble reading.

Over the years, Warner continued to write books for the

> *"I am telling the exact truth when I say that my sister and I began to write when we were just able to hold a pencil."*

Boxcar Children series. She also wrote articles and essays for magazines and newspapers.

Gertrude Chandler Warner died on August 30, 1979, at the age of eighty-nine. Since her death, other authors have continued to write books for the Boxcar Children series, which now boasts more than seventy titles.

⚬

WHERE TO FIND OUT MORE ABOUT GERTRUDE CHANDLER WARNER

BOOKS

Ellsworth, Mary Ellen. *Gertrude Chandler Warner and the Boxcar Children.*
Morton Grove, Ill.: Whitman, 1997.

Wallner, Joan, and Jill Wheeler. *Gertrude Chandler Warner.*
Edina, Minn.: Abdo & Daughters, 1996.

WEB SITES
GRADE 3 BOOK REVIEWS
http://www.crockerfarm.org/meet/reviews3/Contents.htm
To read reviews of Warner's books written by children

KIDSREADS.COM
http://www.kidsreads.com/series/series-boxcar-author.asp
To read biographical information about Warner

———

SEVERAL YEARS AGO, *THE BOXCAR CHILDREN COOKBOOK* WAS PUBLISHED. THE RECIPES WERE INSPIRED BY THE SERIES AND INCLUDE SECRET CODE BUNS, HOBO STEW, AND TREE HOUSE CHOCOLATE PUDDING.

Rosemary Wells

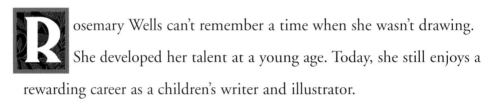

Born: January 29, 1943

Rosemary Wells can't remember a time when she wasn't drawing. She developed her talent at a young age. Today, she still enjoys a rewarding career as a children's writer and illustrator.

Rosemary Wells was born in New York City on January 29, 1943. Her mother was a dancer with the Russian ballet, and her father was a

playwright and actor. Rosemary grew up on the New Jersey shore, and she loved roaming around outdoors as a child. But she loved drawing even more. From the time Rosemary was two years old, her parents encouraged their artistic daughter.

After high school, Rosemary studied art at the Museum School in Boston. But she and the school weren't a good match. When one of her professors told her she was "nothing but an illustrator," she decided she had had enough. She

---

WELLS'S BOOK *READ TO YOUR BUNNY* INSPIRED A NATIONAL CAMPAIGN
TO PROMOTE READING ALOUD TO CHILDREN FROM AN EARLY AGE.

left school, married Tom Wells, and went to work designing children's books.

It wasn't long before Wells stopped designing other people's books and started writing and illustrating her own. She found she had a special talent for creating books for very young readers. These books were simple and short—but they were rich with humor, feeling, and wonderful characters. Noisy Nora, Shy Charles, Stanley and Rhoda, Max and Ruby, Hazel,

> *"Writing for children is as difficult as writing serious verse. Writing for children is as mysterious as writing fine music. It is as personal as singing."*

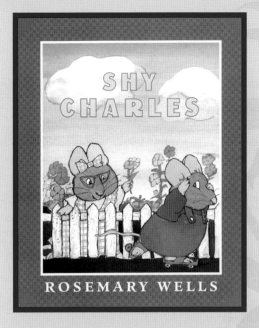

A Selected Bibliography of Wells's Work

The Miraculous Tale of Two Maries (2006)
My Kindergarten (2004)
Felix and the Worrier (2003)
The Secret Birthday (Text only, 2002)
Be My Valentine (Text only, 2001)
Bunny Party (2001)
Emily's First 100 Days of School (2000)
Bunny Cakes (1999)
Here Comes Mother Goose (Illustrations only, 1999)
Read to Your Bunny (1998)
First Tomato (1992)
Max's Dragon Shirt (1991)
Max's Chocolate Chicken (1989)
Shy Charles (1988)
Through the Hidden Door (1987)
Hazel's Amazing Mother (1985)
Timothy Goes to School (1981)
When No One Was Looking (1980)
Stanley & Rhoda (1978)
Benjamin & Tulip (1973)
Noisy Nora (1973)

Wells's Major Literary Award

1989 Boston Globe-Horn Book Picture Book Award
 Shy Charles

> *"Emotion and humor are what make a children's book right. And it's what makes it original, and it's what makes it want to be read again and again. Children's books must be written—published to be read a hundred or two hundred times. The story comes first, the pictures come second."*

Benjamin, and Tulip, Timothy, and Morris—the list of beloved Rosemary Wells characters just goes on and on.

Much of Wells's inspiration has come from her home life. Her West Highland white terriers, have been models for many of her animal characters. And her daughters inspired the Max books and many others. In fact, one reason Wells started making books for very young readers was that she couldn't find anything funny and right to read to her own daughters when they were young. "I wanted to give children adventures they could understand and include jokes parents would recognize," she explains.

Besides writing and illustrating picture and board books, Wells has written novels for middle-schoolers and teenagers. She has also illustrated two huge collections of Mother Goose rhymes. For these, she worked with Iona Opie, a British expert on folk tales and nursery rhymes. Wells loved working on the Mother Goose collections. She says, "Mother Goose herself brought me to a level, spiritually, as an illustrator, that I never knew I could achieve, and now I can't go down from there."

———

PEOPLE OFTEN ASK WELLS WHERE SHE GETS HER IDEAS. SHE ANSWERS, "REALLY WHAT WE DO AS ARTISTS IS FIND. THE IDEAS COME FROM THE CLOUDS, THEY PRE-EXIST."

Rosemary Wells has written and illustrated more than sixty books during her thirty-year career. She has won many awards and has millions of fans. She shows no sign of slowing down. Wells explains, "The job I have now—writing and illustrating children's books—is pure delight. There are hard parts, but no bad or boring parts, and that is more than can be said for any other line of work I know."

✦

WHERE TO FIND OUT MORE ABOUT ROSEMARY WELLS

BOOKS

Kovacs, Deborah, and James Preller. *Meet the Authors and Illustrators: 60 Creators of Favorite Children's Books Talk about Their Work.* Vol. 2. New York: Scholastic, 1993.

Something about the Author. Autobiography Series. Vol. 1. Detroit: Gale Research, 1986.

WEB SITES

HORN BOOKS
http://www.hbook.com/exhibit/wellsradio.html
To read an interview with Rosemary Wells

HOUGHTON MIFFLIN
http://www.eduplace.com/kids/hmr/mtai/wells.html
To read about author and illustrator Rosemary Wells

ROSEMARY WELLS HOME PAGE
http://www.rosemarywells.com/
To visit Rosemary Wells's own Web site

———

WELLS SAYS THAT MANY OF HER BOOKS COME FROM EVERYDAY EVENTS. SHE ADMITS, "AUTHORS ARE ACCOMPLISHED EAVESDROPPERS, AND HAVE WONDERFUL SELECTIVE MEMORY."

E. B. White

Born: July 11, 1899
Died: October 1, 1985

E. B. White wrote only three books for children—but they include the classics *Stuart Little* and *Charlotte's Web*. White also had a long career as a magazine writer and editor.

Elwyn Brooks (E. B.) White was born on July 11, 1899, in Mount Vernon, New York. His father owned a company that manufactured pianos. As a boy, Elwyn was always busy writing. In fact, he began writing as soon as he knew how to spell. "I was no good at drawing, so I used words instead," White once explained. "As I grew older, I found that writing could be a way of earning a living."

IN 1963, WHITE WAS ONE OF THIRTY-ONE AMERICANS TO RECEIVE THE PRESIDENTIAL MEDAL OF FREEDOM FROM PRESIDENT LYNDON B. JOHNSON.

After finishing high school, White attended Cornell University in Ithaca, New York. He served as the editor of the college newspaper.

After he graduated from Cornell in 1921, he worked as a reporter in New York for about a year. Then he and a friend drove across the country. He found a job

> *"I had no intention of writing a book for children, however, and the thing merely grew, by slow stages, over a period of about twelve years. Storytelling does not come easily or naturally to me; I am more of a commentator than a spinner of yarns."*

as a reporter in Seattle, Washington. He worked there for a year before returning to New York City. There, he was hired as a writer for the *New Yorker* magazine, where he remained for the next fifty years, writing poems, essays, and stories. His essays and stories also appeared in several other magazines.

In 1939, White had an idea for a children's book, and he told parts of the story to his nieces and nephews. In 1945, he finished writing his story about the little mouse named Stuart Little.

White and his wife, a *New Yorker* editor, owned a small farm in Maine. He kept animals on his farm and enjoyed spending time in the barn. While watching the animals in the barn, White came up with the idea for another book. "One day when I was on my way to feed the pig, I began feeling

---

NO ONE KNEW WHITE WAS WORKING ON *CHARLOTTE'S WEB*. HIS PUBLISHER WAS SURPRISED WHEN SHE RECEIVED THE MANUSCRIPT.

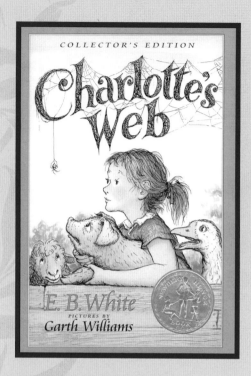

A Selected Bibliography of White's Work

The Trumpet of the Swan (1970)
Charlotte's Web (1952)
Stuart Little (1945)

White's Major Literary Awards

1970 Laura Ingalls Wilder Award
1953 Newbery Honor Book
   Charlotte's Web

sorry for the pig because, like most pigs, he was doomed to die," White remembered. "This made me sad. So I started thinking of ways to save a pig's life." Thinking about the pig inspired him to write *Charlotte's Web,* which was published in 1952.

White did not publish his third book for children until 1970. He decided to write *The*

"Children are a wonderful audience—they are so eager, so receptive, so quick. I have great respect for their powers of observation and reasoning. But like any good writer, I write to amuse myself, not some imaginary audience."

Trumpet of the Swan because of his love of the trumpeter swans he saw at the zoo. The book tells the story of Louis, a swan without a voice.

E. B. White died on October 1, 1985. He was eighty-six years old.

ॐ

WHERE TO FIND OUT MORE ABOUT E. B. WHITE

BOOKS

Agosta, Lucien L. *E. B. White: The Children's Books.*
New York: Twayne Publishing, 1995.

Faber, Doris. *Great Lives: American Literature.* New York:
Atheneum Books for Young Readers, 1995.

Gherman, Beverly. *E. B. White: Some Writer!*
New York: Atheneum Publications, 1992.

McElmeel, Sharron L. *100 Most Popular Children's Authors: Biographical
Sketches and Bibliographies.* Englewood, Colo.: Libraries Unlimited, 1999.

Tingum, Janice. *E. B. White: The Elements of a Writer.*
Minneapolis: Lerner, 1995.

WEB SITES

HARPERCHILDRENS
http://www.harperchildrens.com/catalog/author_xml.asp?authorID=10499
For a biography of E. B. White and an outline of his work

HOUGHTON MIFFLIN READING
http://www.eduplace.com/kids/hmr/mtai/white.html
To read a short biography of E. B. White

WHITE IS THE COAUTHOR OF *THE ELEMENTS OF STYLE.* THIS
BOOK ABOUT WRITING IS USED IN MANY HIGH SCHOOL AND COLLEGE
ENGLISH AND JOURNALISM CLASSES.

David Wiesner

Born: February 5, 1956

When readers enter the wild and wonderful world of a David Wiesner book, they never know where they'll end up. Wiesner writes and illustrates children's picture books, and he loves to create books that tell stories without words. He likes readers to use their own imagination as they travel through his books. Over the years, Wiesner's unique style and interesting way of looking at the world have earned him many awards and honors.

David Wiesner was born in New Jersey on February 5, 1956. He was the youngest of five children. David and his family shared a love of music and art. His parents made sure to keep plenty of art supplies around the house.

Some of David's earliest artistic influences included Bugs Bunny cartoons, *MAD* magazine, and comic books. Later, David read about great artists at his local library. He was especially fascinated by artists

---

WHEN WIESNER WAS A CHILD, HIS FAVORITE THING TO DRAW WAS DINOSAURS.

called surrealists. These artists drew pictures of strange and bizarre things.

Wiesner began his career as an artist while he was still a student at the Rhode Island School of Design. His first paying job was creating a cover illustration for *Cricket,* a children's magazine. Ten years later, Wiesner was asked to create another cover for *Cricket.* This time, he was allowed to draw whatever he liked, and he decided to draw frogs. Later, he created an entire book about frogs, called *Tuesday.*

"A wordless book is a very personal experience for the reader. Each person reads the book differently."

A Selected Bibliography of Wiesner's Work

The Three Pigs (2001)
Sector 7 (1999)
Night of the Gargoyles (Illustrations only, 1994)
Tongues of Jade (Illustrations only, 1991)
Tuesday (1991)
Hurricane (1990)
The Rainbow People (Illustrations only, 1989)
Firebrat (Illustrations only, 1988)
Free Fall (1988)
The Loathsome Dragon (With Kim Kahng, 1987)
The Wand: The Return to Mesmeria (Illustrations only, 1985)
Neptune Rising: Songs and Tales of the Undersea Folk (Illustrations only, 1982)
Owly (Illustrations only, 1982)
The Boy Who Spoke Chimp (Illustrations only, 1981)
The One Bad Thing about Birthdays (Illustrations only, 1981)
The Ugly Princess (Illustrations only, 1981)
Honest Andrew (Illustrations only, 1980)
Man from the Sky (Illustrations only, 1980)

Wiesner's Major Literary Awards

2002 Caldecott Medal
  The Three Pigs
2000 Caldecott Honor Book
  Sector 7
1992 Caldecott Medal
  Tuesday
1989 Caldecott Honor Book
  Free Fall

> *"Growing up in New Jersey, my friends and I re-created our world daily. The neighborhood would become anything from the far reaches of the universe to a prehistoric jungle. To believe that giant pterodactyls were swooping down on us required only a small leap of faith."*

At first, Wiesner illustrated the works of other authors, such as Avi, Eve Bunting, and Jane Yolen. Beginning in 1987, Wiesner began coming up with his own story ideas and illustrating them. One of his first solo projects was *The Loathsome Dragon*. Wiesner and his wife, Kim Kahng, worked on the book together. His next solo project, *Free Fall,* was completely without words.

Many people ask Wiesner where he gets the ideas for his stories. Some ideas come from events in his own life. Wiesner got the idea for *Hurricane,* for example, from a big storm that happened when he was a kid. Lots of Wiesner's ideas come straight from his very active imagination. For instance, he got ideas for *Tuesday* by asking himself, "If I were a frog and I discovered I could fly, where would I go? What would I do?" Wiesner is especially fascinated by flying. Frogs, fish, and even vegetables have flown through his stories!

Wiesner's fantastic imagination and vivid watercolor drawings have earned him a reputation as one of the best children's illustrators

———

IN HIGH SCHOOL, DAVID WIESNER CREATED WORDLESS COMIC BOOKS. ONE OF HIS FIRST WAS CALLED "SLOP THE WONDER PIG." LATER, HE AND HIS FRIENDS MADE A SILENT MOVIE ABOUT VAMPIRES.

today. They have also earned him many awards and honors. Wiesner is a two-time winner of the Caldecott Medal.

In 1997, David Wiesner dove into something new. He created the illustrations for a CD-ROM game called *The Day the World Broke.* The game features flying cows, underground elevators, and talking machines. It was a big hit. No matter what Wiesner draws, his energy and imagination make his work fun for people of all ages.

ॐ

WHERE TO FIND OUT MORE ABOUT DAVID WIESNER

BOOKS

Holtze, Sally Holmes, ed. *Seventh Book of Junior Authors & Illustrators.*
New York: H. W. Wilson Company, 1996.

McElmeel, Sharron L. *100 Most Popular Picture Book Authors and Illustrators: Biographical Sketches and Bibliographies.* Englewood, Colo.: Libraries Unlimited, 2000.

Silvey, Anita, ed. *The Essential Guide to Children's Books and Their Creators.*
Boston: Houghton Mifflin Company, 2002.

WEB SITES

HOUGHTON MIFFLIN BOOKS
http://www.houghtonmifflinbooks.com/authors/wiesner/home.html
For a visual tour of David Wiesner's books

BOOKPAGE
http://www.bookpage.com/9909bp/david_wiesner.html
To read an interview with David Wiesner.

———

WHEN DAVID WIESNER WAS IN FOURTH GRADE, HIS TEACHER SENT AN ANGRY NOTE HOME TO HIS PARENTS. THE NOTE SAID, "DAVID WOULD RATHER BE DRAWING THAN DOING HIS WORK."

Laura Ingalls Wilder

Born: February 7, 1867
Died: February 10, 1957

ost people think of the author Laura Ingalls Wilder as the child in the Little House books. But the person that wrote the books was not a child. Laura Ingalls Wilder didn't publish *Little House in the Big Woods* until she was sixty-five years old! Before that time, she wrote some articles for local newspapers and major magazines. Her daughter, Rose, a professional writer in California, really got her writing seriously. Rose encouraged her mother to write the stories of her childhood experiences.

IN 1954, THE LAURA INGALLS WILDER AWARD WAS CREATED. GIVEN ONCE EVERY TWO YEARS, IT HONORS AN AUTHOR WHO HAS PUBLISHED SEVERAL WORKS IMPORTANT TO THE LIVES OF CHILDREN.

Wilder wrote the books to entertain children and to preserve the stories of what pioneer life on the prairie was like when she was a child. She made sure that each book she wrote was told through the eyes and with the voice of a child.

Laura Ingalls was born on February 7, 1867, in Pepin, Wisconsin. Her parents, Caroline and Charles Ingalls, had four daughters. Laura was the second oldest. Charles Ingalls thought of himself as a pioneer. Like her father, Laura enjoyed moving. She always felt that home was not where a house was, or where she decided to live, but where her family was.

"It is still best to be honest and truthful; to make the most of what we have; to be happy with simple pleasures and to be cheerful and have courage when things go wrong."

"Every American has always been free to pursue his happiness, and so long as Americans are free they will continue to make our country even more wonderful."

The eight books in the Little House series tell the story of her life from when she was a five-year-old living in the Wisconsin woods through her early adult years in De Smet, South Dakota. The books share the experiences of the Ingalls family as Laura's father led them farther into the frontier.

Because they moved many times, Laura went to many schools. Although she never

WILDER DIDN'T HAVE TIME TO WRITE REPLIES TO EVERY PERSON WHO WROTE HER A LETTER. INSTEAD, SHE CAME UP WITH ONE LETTER THAT ANSWERED THE QUESTIONS THAT MOST PEOPLE ASKED HER.

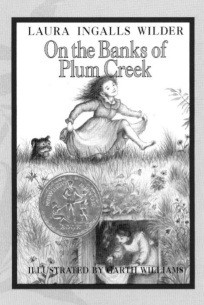

LAURA INGALLS WILDER

On the Banks of Plum Creek

ILLUSTRATED BY GARTH WILLIAMS

A Selected Bibliography of Wilder's Work

The First Four Years (1971)
These Happy Golden Years (1943)
Little Town on the Prairie (1941)
The Long Winter (1940)
By the Shores of Silver Lake (1939)
On the Banks of Plum Creek (1937)
Little House on the Prairie (1935)
Farmer Boy (1933)
Little House in the Big Woods (1932)

Wilder's Major Literary Awards

1954 Laura Ingalls Wilder Award

1944 Newbery Honor Book
   These Happy Golden Years

1942 Newbery Honor Book
   Little Town on the Prairie

1941 Newbery Honor Book
   The Long Winter

1940 Newbery Honor Book
   By the Shores of Silver Lake

1938 Newbery Honor Book
   On the Banks of Plum Creek

graduated from high school, she did earn a teaching certificate in 1882. She took a job in a school several miles from her parents' home. Almost three years later, on August 25, 1885, she married Almanzo Wilder. Laura Ingalls Wilder included their life together in her Little House stories.

Wilder lived in her Mansfield, Missouri, home until February 10, 1957, when she died of a stroke. She received letters from fans around the world right up until the time she died.

It has been more than seventy years since Wilder published *Little House in the Big Woods*. And more than one hundred years have passed since the stories actually took place. But children today continue to read and love the stories of Laura, Mary, Carrie, baby Grace, Ma, and Pa living in the wilderness, experiencing a life that can only be imagined through the words of Laura Ingalls Wilder.

⚬

WHERE TO FIND OUT MORE ABOUT LAURA INGALLS WILDER

BOOKS

Anderson, William. *Laura Ingalls Wilder: A Biography.* New York: HarperCollins, 1992.

Giff, Patricia Reilly. *Laura Ingalls Wilder: Growing Up in the Little House.* New York: Viking Kestrel, 1987.

Greene, Carol. *Laura Ingalls Wilder: Author of the Little House Books.* Chicago: Children's Press, 1990.

McElmeel, Sharron L. *100 Most Popular Children's Authors: Biographical Sketches and Bibliographies.* Englewood, Colo.: Libraries Unlimited, 1999.

Wadsworth, Ginger. *Laura Ingalls Wilder: A Storyteller of the Prairie.* Minneapolis: Lerner, 1996.

WEB SITE

LAURA INGALLS WILDER HOME AND MUSEUM
http://www.lauraingallswilderhome.com/
To read an open letter from Wilder, view pictures of Wilder and her family, and download a map of Wilder's travels

———

IN THE 1970S AND 1980S, A TELEVISION SERIES TITLED *LITTLE HOUSE ON THE PRAIRIE,* BASED ON WILDER'S STORIES, WAS VERY POPULAR. IT STARRED MICHAEL LANDON AS CHARLES INGALLS AND MELISSA GILBERT AS LAURA.

Mo Willems

Born: February 11, 1968

As a former writer for the *Sesame Street* TV show, Mo Willems knows how to make children laugh. "Kids can't fake laughter," says this popular author and illustrator. "So the only way I can judge if what I'm doing is real or true or right is if I can get a laugh."

Mo Willems was born in Chicago, Illinois, shortly after his parents immigrated to the United States from the Netherlands. The family eventually settled in New Orleans, Louisiana, and that's where Mo grew up.

Mo loved reading *Peanuts* comics, and he also admired the clean, simple drawings of *Peanuts* creator Charles Schulz. Mo liked to draw, too, and Schulz's comics inspired him to use simple designs in his own art. His elementary school art teachers did not appreciate his work, though. As he recalls,

WILLEMS WON SIX EMMY AWARDS FOR HIS WRITING ON *SESAME STREET*.

they told him "nothing would ever come of a child who always made silly drawings."

When he got older, Mo enjoyed hanging around New Orleans's blues clubs. As a budding artist, he sketched the scenes he saw. He also told people funny stories. Finding he could make people laugh, he later took to the stage as a stand-up comedian.

Willems attended Tisch School for the Arts at New York University in New York City. At first, he studied filmmaking, but he soon decided to concentrate

"Consciously, all I want to do is make sure that all my books are funny."

A Selected Bibliography of Willems's Work

Don't Let the Pigeon Stay Up Late! (2006)
Leonardo, the Terrible Monster (2005)
Pigeon Has Feelings, Too! (2005)
Time to Say Please! (2005)
Knuffle Bunny: A Cautionary Tale (2004)
Pigeon Finds a Hot Dog! (2004)
Don't Let the Pigeon Drive the Bus! (2003)
Time to Pee! (2003)

Willems's Major Literary Awards

2005 Caldecott Honor Book
    Knuffle Bunny: A Cautionary Tale
2004 Caldecott Honor Book
    Don't Let the Pigeon Drive the Bus!

on animation instead of conventional films. After graduating in 1990, he took a yearlong trip around the world. When he returned, he began getting jobs as an animator, making short animated films for TV.

"Failure is pervasive in children's lives, but I don't know when it stopped being funny. It needs to be explored and enjoyed and laughed at and understood."

In 1993, Willems was hired to work as both a scriptwriter and an animator for the *Sesame Street* TV show. At night, meanwhile, he performed as a stand-up comedian in New York City comedy clubs. After several years at *Sesame Street*, Willems moved to the Cartoon Network. There he created the animated TV series *Sheep in the Big City*. It's about a runaway sheep who leaves the farm for the Big City, where he gets into all kinds of mischief.

Looking for a new challenge, Willems decided to try to publish a children's book. While visiting his agent, he dropped a sketchbook full of scenes that featured a pigeon named Pigeon. The agent saw it and encouraged Willems to put together a Pigeon picture book. It was published in 2003 as *Don't Let the Pigeon Drive the Bus!* Later that year, Willems's picture book *Time to Pee!* came out. It's good-natured look at a common childhood concern. *Pigeon Finds a Hot Dog!* and other Pigeon picture-book adventures followed.

THE WORD *KNUFFLE* (AS IN WILLEMS'S *KNUFFLE BUNNY*) MEANS "SNUGGLE" IN DUTCH, THE LANGUAGE OF THE NETHERLANDS, HIS PARENTS' HOME COUNTRY.

Meanwhile, Willems got married and had a baby daughter named Trixie. Life with Trixie inspired him to write his popular book *Knuffle Bunny: A Cautionary Tale*. It's about a toddler who loses her stuffed bunny on a trip to the laundromat. Willems illustrated the book with cartoon characters. For the backgrounds, he used photos of his own Park Slope neighborhood in New York City's Brooklyn district. Willems still lives there today with Trixie and his wife, Cheryl.

∾

WHERE TO FIND OUT MORE ABOUT MO WILLEMS

WEB SITES

BOOKPAGE
http://www.bookpage.com/0307bp/meet_mo_willems.html
To read Willems's answers to questions about his influences and interests

CURIOUS PICTURES
http://www.curiouspictures.com/commercials/directors_willems.html#
To find a brief biography and clips of film shorts by Willems

MO WILLEMS
http://www.walkerbooks.co.uk/Mo-Willems
For a brief biography and a list of things people don't know about Willems

MO WILLEMS'S STUDIO
http://www.mowillems.com/
To read about the author and his work

———

WILLEMS WAS THE HEAD WRITER FOR THE CARTOON NETWORK'S *CODENAME: KIDS NEXT DOOR.* HE ALSO CREATED THE *OFFBEATS,* A CARTOON SERIES FOR NICKELODEON.

Garth Williams

Born: April 16, 1912
Died: May 8, 1996

Charlotte the spider, Chester Cricket, and Stuart Little are but a few of the famous storybook characters Garth Williams illustrated with pen and ink. Generations of children have fallen in love with the gentle characters he brought to life for some of the most distinguished children's authors of his time—Margaret Wise Brown, George Selden, E. B. White, and Laura Ingalls Wilder. Although Williams wrote seven

children's books of his own, he is better known as an illustrator than as an author.

Garth Montgomery Williams was born in New York City on April 16, 1912. Both of his parents were artists. Garth's father, a cartoonist, drew for *Punch*, a British magazine. His mother was a landscape painter.

WILLIAMS SPENT SEVERAL YEARS ILLUSTRATING LAURA INGALLS WILDER'S
LITTLE HOUSE BOOKS. HE CALLED IT "A MOST EXCITING ADVENTURE."

Garth lived on a farm in New Jersey until the age of ten, when his family moved to England.

In England, Garth Williams studied painting, design, and sculpture at the Westminster Art School and the Royal Academy of Art. When he finished his studies, Williams became head-master of the Luton Art School outside of London. In his spare time, he painted murals.

"Everybody in my home was always either painting or drawing. . . . [I grew up as] a typical Huckleberry Finn, roaming bare-foot around the farm, watching the farmer milk his cows by hand."

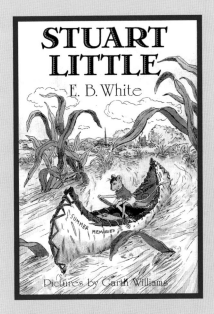

A Selected Bibliography of Williams's Work

Beneath a Blue Umbrella (Illustrations only, 1990)
Over and Over (Illustrations only, 1987)
Self-Portrait: Garth Williams (1982)
Bedtime for Frances (Illustrations only, 1960)
The Rabbits' Wedding (1958)
Baby Farm Animals (1953)
The Little House series (Illustrations only, 1953)
My Bedtime Book (1953)
Baby Animals (1952)
Charlotte's Web (Illustrations only, 1952)
The Adventures of Benjamin Pink (1951)
Stuart Little (Illustrations only, 1945)

"Illustrating books is not just making pictures of the houses, the people and the articles mentioned by the author; the artist has to see everything with the same eyes."

In 1941, Williams returned to the United States, eager to find work. The *New Yorker* magazine hired him as a cartoonist and illustrator. While there, he illustrated E. B. White's book *Stuart Little,* which launched his career as a children's book illustrator. In this first work for children, Williams showcased his ability to create characters that looked like animals but walked and talked like humans. He kept this style in later books, giving each animal a human personality with hopes and dreams.

In 1952, Williams worked with E. B. White on another book, *Charlotte's Web,* the story of a spider who saves a pig's life. It has since become a classic in children's literature.

During the 1950s, Williams also illustrated eight of Laura Ingalls Wilder's Little House books about the American frontier. His illustrations depict what pioneer life was like for the Ingalls family, who lived in the forests of Wisconsin and on the prairies of Kansas, Minnesota, and Dakota Territory.

Williams continued illustrating children's books during the 1980s. His long, successful career came to an end on May 8, 1996, when he died of cancer at his home in Guanajuato, Mexico.

———

GARTH WILLIAMS HAD FOUR WIVES, FIVE DAUGHTERS, AND ONE SON. HIS FIRST DAUGHTER, FIONA, WAS HIS MODEL FOR FERN, THE LITTLE GIRL IN THE BOOK *CHARLOTTE'S WEB.*

Always a respectful illustrator, Garth Williams worked well with authors. He had discovered early in his career how to see events and characters through an author's eyes. This gift enabled him to please his authors and fascinate his readers. For more than fifty years, his warmhearted characters have delighted children of all ages.

❧

WHERE TO FIND OUT MORE ABOUT GARTH WILLIAMS

BOOKS

Silvey, Anita, ed. *The Essential Guide to Children's Books and Their Creators.*
Boston: Houghton Mifflin Company, 2002.

Something about the Author. Autobiography Series.
Vol. 7. Detroit: Gale Research, 1989.

Williams, Garth. *Self-Portrait: Garth Williams.*
Boston: Addison Wesley Longman, 1982.

WEB SITES

BIOGRAPHY
http://webpages.marshall.edu/~irby1/laura/garth.html
To read a biography of Garth

HARPER COLLINS CHILDREN
*http://www.harpercollinschildrens.com/HarperChildrens/Kids/
AuthorsAndIllustrators/ContributorDetail.aspx?CId=12897*
For a short biography about the author

MOST OF WILLIAMS'S ILLUSTRATIONS FOR GRADE-SCHOOL CHILDREN
WERE DONE IN BLACK AND WHITE. AT THE TIME, PUBLISHING BOOKS IN
COLOR WAS VERY COSTLY.

Vera B. Williams

Born: January 28, 1927

Vera B. Williams has lived on a houseboat, worked as a cook, and opened a school. Then when she was in her forties, she settled into her present profession—author and illustrator of picture books for children.

Williams was born Vera Baker in 1927 in Hollywood, California. During her childhood, her family moved to New York City's Bronx neighborhood. "Mine was a fiercely scrapping, loud-talking, loving but unsettled family struggling to make a living," she says. Many of those family struggles would later be reflected in her books.

Vera's parents taught their two daughters to care about social issues. They also encouraged the girls to develop their artistic talents. Vera studied art, and one of her paintings was exhibited at the Museum of Modern Art in New York City. Just nine years old at the time, she was thrilled when first lady Eleanor Roosevelt attended the exhibit. Vera had the honor of explaining her painting and answering Roosevelt's questions.

DURING HER TIME AT THE MUSIC AND ART HIGH SCHOOL IN NEW YORK CITY, VERA CREATED HER OWN HANDMADE BOOKS.

She later attended Black Mountain College in North Carolina and majored in graphic art. This was where she met Paul Williams, who was studying to be an architect. They married and together helped to build the Gate Hill Cooperative. This was a community of artists and musicians in Stony Point, New York. The Williamses' three children—Sarah, Jennifer, and Merce—grew up there.

Williams and other community residents also opened an alternative school, where she enjoyed teaching arts

"As a person who works for children, who raised three children . . . I have to be able to say I did something to try to save our planet from destruction. It is my faith that we will."

and crafts. For one project, she and her class built gingerbread houses. She would draw those fanciful houses later in her book *It's a Gingerbread House: Bake It, Build It, Eat It!* in 1978.

Williams's marriage ended in 1970, and she moved to Canada. She made her home in a houseboat on the bay at Vancouver, British Columbia. It was here that she began writing and illustrating children's books. Williams loved the Canadian wilderness, and she once took an adventurous canoe trip down the Yukon River. Many of her boating experiences appear in *Three Days on a River in a Red Canoe*, which was

WILLIAMS CURRENTLY LIVES IN NEW YORK CITY.

A Selected Bibliography of Williams's Work

Amber Was Brave, Essie Was Smart (2001)

Lucky Song (1997)

Scooter (1993)

"More More More," Said the Baby (1990)

Cherries and Cherry Pits (1986)

Music, Music for Everyone (1984)

Something Special for Me (1983)

A Chair for My Mother (1981)

Three Days on a River in a Red Canoe (1981)

It's a Gingerbread House: Bake It, Build It, Eat It! (1978)

Williams's Major Literary Awards

2002 Boston Globe-Horn Book Fiction Honor Book
   Amber Was Brave, Essie Was Smart

1994 Boston Globe-Horn Book Fiction Award
   Scooter

1991 Caldecott Honor Book
   "More More More," Said the Baby

1988 Boston Globe-Horn Book Picture Book Honor Book
   Stringbean's Trip to the Shining Sea

1987 Boston Globe-Horn Book Picture Book Honor Book
   Cherries and Cherry Pits

1983 Boston Globe-Horn Book Picture Book Award
1983 Caldecott Honor Book
   A Chair for My Mother

published eleven years after her arrival in Canada.

Community and family are major themes in Williams's books. A Hispanic girl named Rosa is the main character in three beloved stories—*A Chair for My Mother*, *Something Special for Me*, and *Music, Music for Everyone*. These titles reveal Rosa's loving relationship with her struggling family. The girls in *Amber Was Brave, Essie Was Smart* have a special kind of family problem: their father is in prison. Still, they handle the situation with sensitivity and love.

Williams never lost the social consciousness her parents instilled in her. She lends her support to many causes, including women's and children's rights, peace, and the environment. She has even been arrested for taking part in demonstrations. One arrest led to a month's stay in a federal prison in 1981. For Williams, her efforts are simply part of trying to make the world a better place.

"The people I show in my books are like the people I grew up with in many different neighborhoods. . . . Trying to get by from week to week was a major part of life for them."

WHERE TO FIND OUT MORE ABOUT VERA B. WILLIAMS

BOOKS

McElmeel, Sharron L. *100 Most Popular Picture Book Authors and Illustrators: Biographical Sketches and Bibliographies*. Englewood, Colo.: Libraries Unlimited, 2000.

Pendergast, Sara, and Tom Pendergast, eds. *St. James Guide to Children's Writers*. 5th ed. Detroit: St. James Press, 1999.

Silvey, Anita, ed. *The Essential Guide to Children's Books and Their Creators*. Boston: Houghton Mifflin Company, 2002.

WEB SITES

BOOK WIRE
http://www.bookwire.com/bookwire/MeettheAuthor/Interview_Vera_Williams.htm
To read an interview with Vera B. Williams

HARPERCOLLINS
http://www.harperchildrens.com/catalog/author_xml.asp?authorid=19040
To read an article about why Williams wanted to be an author

WILLIAMS ONCE COOKED AND RAN THE BAKERY AT EVERDALE SCHOOL IN THE COUNTRYSIDE OF ONTARIO, CANADA.

David Wisniewski

Born: March 21, 1953
Died: September 12, 2002

Some people seem to be born knowing they want to be authors. Others make discoveries along the way that lead them to that career. It would be hard to find a better example of that process of discovery than David Wisniewski, who became an author and illustrator by first being a clown and a puppeteer.

David Wisniewski was born on March 21, 1953. His father was in the U.S. military, and the family lived in England, Nebraska, Texas, and Germany while David was growing up. Wisniewski wanted to study theater but he ran out of money after one semester in college. He learned that the Ringling Brothers and Barnum & Bailey Circus would pay him to go to its clown college, so he signed up. He learned acrobatics and

DAVID WISNIEWSKI'S FIRST BOOK AS AN ILLUSTRATOR, *DUCKY,* IS BASED ON A NEWS STORY ABOUT A CRATE OF **29,000** RUBBER DUCKIES WASHED OVERBOARD FROM A CARGO SHIP IN A STORM.

juggling, as well as how to ride a unicycle. He then spent three years as a clown for Ringling and for Circus Vargas.

When circus life got tiring, Wisniewski took what he knew about performing and got a job at a puppet theater. His boss, Donna Harris, soon became his wife. Their specialty was shadow puppetry—in which flat figures of cut-out paper cast shadows on a screen. When they had children and wanted to stop touring, the couple started a graphic-design company.

Wisniewski met a former children's book editor who was so impressed with his work that she gave him the name of an editor and told him to visit her right away. Wisniewski didn't. He spent months planning. When he finally went to see the editor, he had a story and several finished illustrations.

> *"I think if you truly want to do something—you can. The problem is—in art or any discipline—one gets discouraged and stops. When I pursue something difficult, I often keep in mind something former president Calvin Coolidge said: 'Everything yields to diligence.'"*

That story became his first book, *The Warrior and the Wise Man.* Set in Japan, it is the adventure of two samurai brothers—one brave, and one wise. The book has two Wisniewski trademarks.

First, the story was written to fit in with real Japanese legends. Wisniewski carefully researched the customs and beliefs of the people he

REAL CLOWNS IN THE CIRCUS PAINT BIG RED MOUTHS ONLY ON THEIR LOWER LIPS, SAID WISNIEWSKI. YOU CAN SEE IT IN THE ILLUSTRATIONS HE DREW FOR *AMANDA JOINS THE CIRCUS*, BY AVI.

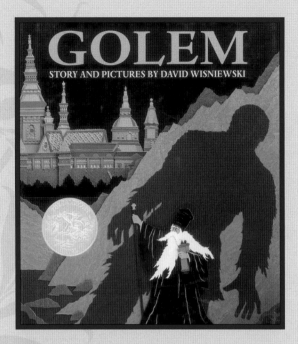

A Selected Bibliography of Wisniewski's Work

Master Man: A Tall Tale of Nigeria (Illustrations only, 2001)
The Secret Knowledge of Grown-Ups: The Second File (2001)
I'll Play with You (Illustrations only, 2000)
Amanda Joins the Circus (Illustrations only, 1999)
Keep Your Eye on Amanda (Illustrations only, 1999)
Tough Cookie (1999)
Workshop (Illustrations only, 1999)
The Secret Knowledge of Grown-Ups (1998)
Ducky (Illustrations only, 1997)
Golem (1996)
The Wave of the Sea-Wolf (1994)
Sundiata: Lion King of Mali (1992)
Rain Player (1991)
Elfwyn's Saga (1990)
The Warrior and the Wise Man (1989)

Wisniewski's Major Literary Award

1997 Caldecott Medal
  Golem

wrote about. He wrote folktales set in Africa *(Sundiata: Lion King of Mali)*, ancient Iceland *(Elfwyn's Saga)*, and North America's Mayan and Tlingit cultures *(Rain Player* and *The Wave of the Sea-Wolf)*.

Second, *The Warrior and the Wise Man* displays Wisniewski's trademark style of art. From his days working with shadow puppets, Wisniewski was skilled in making illustrations out of cut paper. Each illustration contains up to twelve layers of paper. Wisniewski did his cutting with small knives. He wore out about 800 blades for each book.

In 1997, Wisniewski won the Caldecott Medal for *Golem*, a dark tale about a clay giant brought to life to guard a Jewish ghetto of long-ago Prague. Until his death on September 12, 2002, Wisniewski continued to think of writing for children as a serious calling. "What a privilege!" he said. "What a responsibility!"

> *"I try to create richly detailed, obsessively accurate, original folktales set in ancient cultures, but with modern messages. I consider the work my ministry; my service to others."*

❧

WHERE TO FIND OUT MORE ABOUT DAVID WISNIEWSKI

BOOKS

Holtze, Sally Holmes, ed. *Seventh Book of Junior Authors & Illustrators.* New York: H. W. Wilson Company, 1996.

McElmeel, Sharron L. *100 Most Popular Children's Authors: Biographical Sketches and Bibliographies.* Englewood, Colo.: Libraries Unlimited, 1999.

WEB SITES

AUTHOR SPOTLIGHT
http://www.eduplace.com/rdg/author/wisniewski/
To read an interview with David Wisniewski

ILLUSTRATED BOOKS BY DAVID WISNIEWSKI
http://scils.rutgers.edu/~kvander/golem/davidw.html
To see examples of Wisniewski's work

WISNIEWSKI HAD NO FORMAL ART TRAINING. HE JOKED THAT HE WENT TO "THE STAN LEE SCHOOL OF ARTISTS"—MEANING THAT HE STUDIED ART BY LOOKING AT THE DRAWINGS IN MARVEL COMICS, PUBLISHED BY STAN LEE.

Virginia Euwer Wolff

Born: August 25, 1937

"My fictional characters confront experiences that confuse and often disorient them," says Virginia Euwer Wolff. Many young readers readily identify with those characters. Wolff's young-adult novels offer a vision of hope, though. Although her characters make mistakes, they find their own strength and manage to prevail over difficult circumstances.

Virginia Euwer was born in Portland, Oregon, in 1937. She lived with her parents and older brother in a log cabin in the Oregon woods. There the family ran a pear and apple farm. Towering in the distance were Mount Hood and other snowcapped peaks. As a child, Virginia swam in mountain lakes, picked strawberries, and drank fresh milk from the family cow. A huge fireplace warmed their cozy home, and the children were surrounded with paintings, classical

---

FROM 1986 TO 1998, WOLFF TAUGHT ENGLISH AT OREGON'S MOUNT HOOD ACADEMY, A HIGH SCHOOL FOR COMPETITIVE SKIERS.

music, and books. Virginia's favorite reading material was *Winnie-the-Pooh*.

Her happy life was shattered at age five when her father died. Still, her mother tried to keep the children inspired with educational experiences. On family trips to New York City, Virginia discovered museums and the theater. She loved the world of music and, at age eight, began

> "*Each book pushes me farther out on an intellectual and emotional limb. . . . My fascination with what we humans do when we learn the consequences of our own behavior keeps me writing.*"

A Selected Bibliography of Wolff's Work

True Believer (2001)
Bat 6 (1998)
Make Lemonade (1993)
The Mozart Season (1991)
Probably Still Nick Swansen (1988)
Rated PG (1981)

studying the violin. As she grew older, her reading tastes turned to comic books and Nancy Drew mysteries.

When Virginia was sixteen, her mother sent her off to a boarding school for girls. After graduation, she enrolled in Smith College in Northampton, Massachusetts, earning a degree in English in 1959. The summer after graduation, she married Art Wolff. They had two children, Anthony and Juliet.

Art worked in the theater, and the family moved around as he went from one job to another. Over the course of seventeen years, they moved twelve times. Virginia taught school in many cities, including New York City's Bronx neighborhood; Philadelphia, Pennsylvania; and Glen Cove on New York's Long Island.

When her kids were teenagers, Wolff decided to try her hand at writing. In 1974, she began working on a master's degree in creative writing at Long Island University, but she dropped out before finishing. After she and her husband divorced in 1976, she returned to Oregon with her children. There she taught high school English in the town of Hood River. She began writing in earnest, too. Her first

> *"I'm always listening to classical music while I'm writing. . . . If I don't have music, I'm half a brain."*

WOLFF HAS PLAYED THE VIOLIN WITH THE MID-COLUMBIA SINFONIETTA OF PORTLAND, OREGON, AS WELL AS OTHER ORCHESTRAL GROUPS.

young-adult novel, *Probably Still Nick Swansen*, was published in 1988. It's about the struggles of a teenager with learning disabilities.

Wolff's love for music is obvious in her next book, *The Mozart Season*. It follows the joys and heartbreaks of a twelve-year-old violinist who is preparing for a competition. *Make Lemonade* is the story of four-teen-year-old LaVaughn, who lives in a housing project. LaVaughn reappears, slightly older, in *True Believer*. Both books are written in a kind of free verse, with lines of varying length. In between these two books, Wolff published *Bat 6*. It's about the girls who make up a softball team in the 1940s and the prejudice they face.

Today, Wolff lives in Oregon City, Oregon, where she writes from her home in the woods.

❧

WHERE TO FIND OUT MORE ABOUT VIRGINIA EUWER WOLFF

BOOKS
Reid, Suzanne Elizabeth. Virginia Euwer Wolff: *Capturing the Music of Young Voices.*
Lanham, Md.: The Scarecrow Press, 2003.

WEB SITES
SCHOLASTIC
http://books.scholastic.com/teachers/authorsandbooks/authorstudies/authorhome.jsp?authorID=17
67&displayName=Biography
For a brief biography of the author

———

MAKE LEMONADE AND *TRUE BELIEVER* WERE THE FIRST TWO BOOKS
IN WOLFF'S MAKE LEMONADE TRILOGY.

Audrey Wood
Don Wood

Born: 1948 (Audrey)
Born: May 4, 1945 (Don)

Audrey and Don Wood work together on their children's books. Audrey comes up with an idea for a book. She then shares it with Don to see if he wants to illustrate it. Sometimes he does the illustrations, and other times they decide to have Audrey illustrate the book. After being married for more than three decades, they just know who should illustrate each project. The Woods have worked on many books together, including *The Napping House, King Bidgood's in the Bathtub,* and *Jubal's Wish.* Audrey has also written and illustrated many of her own books.

Audrey Wood was born in 1948 in Little Rock, Arkansas. There were many artists in her family, including

---

IN HIS JOB WITH THE CIRCUS, AUDREY WOOD'S FATHER PAINTED THE MURALS FOR THE BIG TOP AND THE SIDESHOWS.

both her father and grandfather. When she was a toddler, Audrey and her family lived in Florida. Her father worked as a painter for the Ringling Brothers and Barnum & Bailey Circus. Her family then moved to Mexico, where her parents studied art.

As a child, Audrey took lessons in dance, drama, and art. She knew that she wanted to be an artist.

> "I would open one of my parents' lavishly illustrated art books and make up stories about the paintings. The nature encyclopedia was also one of our favorites, especially the section on reptiles and amphibians."
> —Audrey Wood

A Selected Bibliography of the Woods' Work

Alphabet Rescue (Illustrations by Bruce Wood, 2006)
Magic Shoelaces (2005)
Ten Little Fish (Illustrations by Bruce Wood, 2004)
Piggy Pie Po (2003)
Princess and the Dragon (2002)
Alphabet Adventure (Illustrations by Bruce Wood, 2001)
Jubal's Wish (2000)
Bright and Early Thursday Evening: A Tangled Tale (1996)
Silly Sally (1992)
Piggies (1991)
Oh My Baby Bear! (1990)
Weird Parents (1989)
Elbert's Bad Word (1988)
Heckedy Peg (1987)
King Bidgood's in the Bathtub (1985)
The Napping House (1984)
Moonflute (1980)

The Woods' Major Literary Award

1986 Caldecott Honor Book
  King Bidgood's in the Bathtub

> *"A picture book is at least half theater or half film. Rhythm is an extremely important element. Also critical is point of view. . . . Maybe because we've both worked in theater . . . we're sensitive to split-second nuances that can make or break a show, or a picture book. For us, the page is a stage."*
>
> *—Don Wood*

Don Wood was born on May 4, 1945, in Atwater, California. He grew up on a farm where peaches, oranges, grapes, almonds, and sweet potatoes were grown. Don worked very hard. When he was in sixth grade, he was put in charge of forty acres of the farm.

Don loved to draw, but he was too busy on the farm most of the time. "Winter was my time to draw," Wood remembers, "so I did constantly." Like his future wife, he too knew that he wanted to be an artist when he grew up.

Audrey and Don met in California in the 1960s when they were both studying art. They were married in 1969, and soon thereafter, they traveled to Mexico and Guatemala. They brought home pottery and sculpture made by indigenous Mexican artists. They used it to open an art shop in Arkansas.

After their son was born, Audrey decided to make a career change. She wanted to become a children's book author. She thought that it would be best for them to move to New York City because

TO MAKE HIS DRAWINGS MORE REALISTIC, DON WOOD OFTEN USES HUMAN MODELS FOR HIS PICTURES. BOTH HIS WIFE AND THEIR SON, BRUCE, HAVE MODELED FOR HIM.

there were many publishers there. Instead, Don convinced her to move to California.

The first book that Audrey and Don Wood worked on together was *Moonflute.* Audrey wrote the story, and Don created the illustrations. Since then, they have written and illustrated more than ten books together. Audrey and Don Wood continue to create children's books. They live in Santa Barbara, California.

❧

WHERE TO FIND OUT MORE ABOUT AUDREY AND DON WOOD

BOOKS

Holtze, Sally Holmes, ed. *Sixth Book of Junior Authors & Illustrators.*
New York: H .W. Wilson Company, 1989.

McElmeel, Sharron L. *100 Most Popular Picture Book Authors and Illustrators: Biographical Sketches and Bibliographies.* Englewood, Colo.: Libraries Unlimited, 2000.

Silvey, Anita, ed. *The Essential Guide to Children's Books and Their Creators.*
Boston: Houghton Mifflin Company, 2002.

Something about the Author. Vol. 50. Detroit: Gale Research, 1988.

WEB SITES
AUDREY WOOD HOME PAGE
http://www.audreywood.com/
For information on Audrey Wood's past, current, and upcoming projects

HARCOURT BOOKS
http://www.harcourtbooks.com/authorinterviews/bookinterview_Wood.asp
To read an interview with Audrey and Don Wood.

WHEN HE WAS A YOUNG BOY, DON WOOD COULD NOT FIND PAPER LARGE ENOUGH FOR HIS DRAWINGS. HE WOULD USE THE PAPER THAT THE FAMILY'S LAUNDRY CAME WRAPPED IN.

Jacqueline Woodson

Born: February 12, 1964

As she was growing up, Jacqueline Woodson often felt that she didn't fit in. Now she writes about young people on the fringes of mainstream society. They are the ones who often go unnoticed, yet they struggle to find their value as individuals.

Jacqueline Amanda Woodson was born in Columbus, Ohio, in 1964. With her sister and two brothers, she spent her early years in Greenville, South Carolina. When Jacqueline was about seven years old, the family moved to Brooklyn in New York City. There her neighbors were mostly Hispanic and African American, and she grew up experiencing the food and music of both cultures.

Even as a child, Jacqueline loved to write. She wrote stories on paper bags and sidewalks. She even wrote on her own shoes. Once she wrote her name on the side of a building. This got her into trouble, though.

WHEN JACQUELINE WAS A TODDLER, SHE APPEARED IN ADVERTISEMENTS FOR ALAGA SYRUP IN *EBONY* MAGAZINE.

"One of the most important ideas I want to get across to my readers is the idea of feeling like you're okay with who you are."

In school, Jacqueline was not very good at math or science. Her favorite subjects were gym, Spanish, and English. When she was in fifth grade, she became the literary editor of her school magazine. This gave her the opportunity to write articles on many subjects.

Jacqueline's seventh-grade teacher encouraged her to keep writing and to pursue a career in whatever made her happy. "I used to say I'd be a teacher or a lawyer or a hairdresser when I grew up," she recalls, "but even as I said these things, I knew what made me happiest was writing." So she decided to be a writer. She wanted to write about situations familiar to her, such as African American communities, friendship, and girlhood.

When Jacqueline was a teenager, she lived part of the time in South Carolina and part of the time in Brooklyn. As a result, she felt like an outsider no matter where she was. This made her sympathetic to outsiders of all kinds, and she later wrote about the struggles of people who feel out of place.

Woodson attended Adelphi University in Garden City, New York, earning a bachelor's

"Every character I write about is in some way outside of the mainstream—black, working-class poor white, a pregnant teen, gay."

WOODSON STUDIED CREATIVE WRITING AT NEW YORK CITY'S NEW SCHOOL FOR SOCIAL RESEARCH.

A Selected Bibliography of Woodson's Work

Show Way (2005)

Behind You (2004)

Coming on Home Soon (2004)

Dear One (2004)

Locomotion (2003)

Hush (2002)

Our Gracie Aunt (2002)

Visiting Day (2002)

Other Side (2001)

Miracle's Boys (2000)

Sweet, Sweet Memory (2000)

Lena (1999)

If You Come Softly (1998)

The House You Pass on the Way (1997)

We Had a Picnic This Sunday Past (1997)

Autobiography of a Family Photo (1995)

From the Notebooks of Melanin Sun (1995)

I Hadn't Meant to Tell You This (1994)

Between Madison and Palmetto (1993)

Maizon at Blue Hill (1992)

Last Summer with Maizon (1990)

Martin Luther King Jr. and His Birthday (1990)

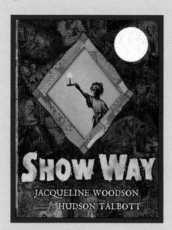

Woodson's Major Literary Awards

2006 Newbery Honor Book
Show Way

2004 Coretta Scott King Author Honor Book
2003 Boston Globe–Horn Book Fiction and Poetry Honor Book
Locomotion

2001 Coretta Scott King Author Award
Miracle's Boys

1996 Coretta Scott King Author Honor Book
From the Notebooks of Melanin Sun

1995 Coretta Scott King Author Honor Book
I Hadn't Meant to Tell You This

degree in English in 1985. After college, she held a variety of jobs, including working as a drama therapist with runaway and homeless kids in New York City's Harlem district. Meanwhile, she kept working at her writing.

Woodson found she was especially interested in writing about young girls and their problems with self-esteem. She published her first book, *Last Summer with Maizon*, in 1990. It follows the friendship of two African American girls as both face upheavals in their lives. The two girls appear again in *Maizon at Blue Hill* and *Between Madison and Palmetto*.

In each of her books, Woodson faces difficult themes head-on. *If You Come Softly, I*

Hadn't Meant to Tell You This, and *Lena* address the problems of inter-racial friendships. Young people struggle with issues of homosexuality in *From the Notebooks of Melanin Sun* and *The House You Pass on the Way*. Other books deal with abuse, alcoholism, teenage pregnancy, and relationships between rich and poor African Americans.

Woodson and her daughter, Toshi, live in Brooklyn.

⁂

WHERE TO FIND OUT MORE ABOUT JACQUELINE WOODSON

BOOKS

Silvey, Anita, ed. *The Essential Guide to Children's Books and Their Creators.*
Boston: Houghton Mifflin Company, 2002.

Stover, Lois Thomas. *Jacqueline Woodson: The Real Thing.*
Metuchen, N.J.: Scarecrow Press, 2004.

WEB SITES

JACQUELINE WOODSON HOME PAGE
http://www.jacquelinewoodson.com/
For a biography, list of books, and awards

BOOKLIST
http://usinfo.state.gov/usa/blackhis/bkl05-interview.htm
To read an interview with Woodson

HOUGHTON MIFFLIN READING
http://www.eduplace.com/kids/hmr/mtai/woodson.html
For a brief article about Woodson

———

WOODSON'S BOOK *MIRACLE'S BOYS*, ABOUT THREE ORPHANED BROTHERS IN NEW YORK, WAS MADE INTO A TV MINISERIES IN 2005.

Betty Ren Wright

Born: June 15, 1927

Almost all children are thrilled by a scary story. That is one reason why author Betty Ren Wright is so popular. Wright is a children's book author, and many of her books are ghost stories and mysteries. Some of her books include *The Doll-house Murders, Christina's Ghost,* and *The Pike River Phantom.*

Wright was born on June 15, 1927, in Wakefield, Michigan. Both her father and her mother were teachers. Betty enjoyed writing as a child. She says, "My first book was a collection of poems begun when I was

---

BETTY REN WRIGHT'S SHORT STORIES HAVE BEEN PUBLISHED IN *REDBOOK, LADIES' HOME JOURNAL,* AND *COSMOPOLITAN.*

> *"I was blessed with teachers in grade school, high school, and college who encouraged me a great deal."*

seven. My mother bought a black loose-leaf notebook, had my name lettered on it, and there it was—a dream come true, a dream that I wanted to repeat."

Throughout school, teachers encouraged Betty to write, and they also gave her some advice. They told her to have another job while she was writing so that she would have a regular paycheck.

After she graduated from high school, Wright attended what is now Lawrence University of Wisconsin. She remembered the advice of her teachers. When she had earned her college degree, she got a job as an editorial assistant. She worked with authors to publish their writing.

Meanwhile, Wright wrote her own stories in her free time. Most of these stories were short fiction for adults. Finally, in 1978, she decided to quit her editing job and become a full-time writer.

Wright planned to focus on fiction for adults. But first, she decided to write one story for young readers. It was

> *"Each of my books has sizeable chunks of my own life in it— people or events or feelings, or all three."*

IN 1954, WRIGHT PUBLISHED *MR. MOGGS' DOGS* UNDER THE NAME REVENA, WHICH IS HER MOTHER'S NAME.

A Selected Bibliography of Wright's Work

Princess for a Week (2006)

The Blizzard (2003)

Crandall's Castle (2003)

The Moonlight Man (2000)

The Wish Master (2000)

A Ghost in the Family (1998)

The Cat Next Door (1991)

The Pike River Phantom (1988)

Christina's Ghost (1985)

Ghosts beneath Our Feet (1984)

The Dollhouse Murders (1983)

The Secret Window (1982)

Getting Rid of Marjorie (1981)

Good Morning, Farm (1964)

Poppyseed (1954)

Yellow Cat (1952)

Willy Woo-oo-oo (1951)

called *Getting Rid of Marjorie.* She enjoyed it so much that she decided to write one more for children. Then, she wrote another and another. Today, she's still writing stories for children.

"I love being scared!" Wright says. So it is not a surprise that many of her books are ghost stories and mysteries.

The ideas for Wright's stories come from events and experiences in her own life. She gets ideas from things she sees in the park, people in her life, and places she has visited. She wrote about a boy, Charlie Hocking, in *The Pike River Phantom* because someone asked her why all her books were about girls.

Betty Ren Wright gives speeches about her work and

often conducts workshops. She continues to write novels and short stories for children and adults. "The best moments of all come when I hear from boys and girls who have enjoyed what I had to tell," says Wright. "Until a reader says 'I like it!' writing a book is a little like talking into an empty room." She lives in Kenosha, Wisconsin, with her husband, George Frederiksen, who is an artist.

❧

WHERE TO FIND OUT MORE ABOUT BETTY REN WRIGHT

BOOKS

Holtze, Sally Holmes, ed. *Sixth Book of Junior Authors & Illustrators.* New York: H. W. Wilson Company, 1989.

McElmeel, Sharron L. *100 Most Popular Children's Authors: Biographical Sketches and Bibliographies.* Englewood, Colo.: Libraries Unlimited, 1999.

WEB SITE

OUTLINE OF THE MOONLIGHT MAN
http://www.secondaryenglish.com/moonlightman.html
For information about Betty Ren Wright's book
The Moonlight Man

WRIGHT'S STORIES HAVE BEEN PUBLISHED IN DANISH, SPANISH, AND SWEDISH.

Laurence Yep

Born: June 14, 1948

Laurence Yep grew up in San Francisco, California, surrounded by three cultures—white, black, and Asian. Yet he never really felt a part of any one of them, even though he is Chinese American. When he entered high school, he felt ignored by the other students. So, in his quiet way, he fought back. He began writing works of science fiction and filled them with places and characters unlike any he had known before. In his own made-up universe, life could work out just the way Yep wanted.

Laurence Yep was born on June 14, 1948, in San Francisco. He published his first science fiction story when he was just eighteen. After graduating from college, he published his first book, *Sweetwater,* about an early colonist from planet Earth who visits a star called Harmony.

LATER GATOR WAS INSPIRED BY A REAL-LIFE REPTILE. WHEN YEP WAS YOUNGER, HE KEPT A PET ALLIGATOR NAMED OSCAR.

After this early success, Yep decided to explore his Chinese heritage. His ideas about his grandparents' homeland came from stories he had been told as a child. In this China, there was no Great Wall or Imperial Palace, only small villages filled with people who longed to go to America—the "Golden Mountain"—to work and become rich. For Yep, Chinese legends and myths mixed together with tales of real life.

"I get the ideas from everything. Children sometimes think you have to have special experiences to write, but good writing brings out what's special in ordinary things."

A Selected Bibliography of Yep's Work

Tiger Magic (2006)

Skunk Scout (2003)

Spring Pearl: The Last Flower (2002)

Angelfish (2001)

Dream Soul (2000)

The Magic Paintbrush (2000)

The Amah (1999)

The Imp That Ate My Homework (1998)

Later Gator (1995)

Dragon's Gate (1993)

The Man Who Tricked a Ghost (1993)

Dragon Cauldron (1991)

The Star Fisher (1991)

Tongues of Jade (1991)

The Rainbow People (1989)

Dragon Steel (1985)

Dragon of the Lost Sea (1982)

Child of the Owl (1977)

Dragonwings (1975)

Sweetwater (1973)

Yep's Major Literary Awards

2005 Laura Ingalls Wilder Award

1994 Newbery Honor Book
Dragon's Gate

1989 Boston Globe-Horn Book Nonfiction Honor Book
The Rainbow People

1977 Boston Globe-Horn Book Fiction Award
Child of the Owl

1976 Boston Globe-Horn Book Fiction Honor Book

1976 Carter G. Woodson Book Award

1976 Newbery Honor Book
Dragonwings

> *"Probably the reason why much of my writing has found its way to a teenage audience is that I'm always pursuing the theme of being an outsider—an alien—and many teenagers feel they're aliens. All of my books have dealt with the outsider."*

Dragonwings, published in 1975, tells the story of a young Chinese man, Moon Shadow, who travels to America to be with his father, Windrider.

Many of the characters in *Dragonwings,* which was named a Newbery Honor Book, were included in *Dragon's Gate,* a story about people struggling to live within two very different cultures.

In *The Star Fisher,* Yep returns to another place he had heard about over and over as a child. His mother was born in Ohio but spent much of her childhood in Clarksburg, West Virginia. Her father—Laurence's grandfather—had opened a laundry there. The family became the first Asians to live in Clarksburg. Joan Lee, the heroine of *The Star Fisher,* is much like Yep's own mother. She feels the pain of racism but also the joy of seeing and learning new things.

In retelling the stories he heard from his parents and grandparents, Laurence Yep writes history colored by memory. Yep has not, however, forgotten his first love of science fiction and fantasy. His works include *Dragon of the Lost Sea* and *Dragon Cauldron.* He has also retold

---

YEP TELLS YOUNG WRITERS TO USE ALL OF THEIR SENSES AS PART OF THE "CREATIVE PROCESS." HE SAYS TOO MANY WRITERS "JUST USE THEIR EYES."

Chinese legends and folktales. Once a boy who believed he wasn't part of any one culture, Yep has become an expert guide to unknown worlds, both alien and earthbound.

❧

WHERE TO FIND OUT MORE ABOUT LAURENCE YEP

BOOKS

Drew, Bernard A. *The 100 Most Popular Young Adult Authors: Biographical Sketches and Bibliographies.* Englewood, Colo.: Libraries Unlimited, 1997.

Johnson-Feelings, Dianne. *Presenting Laurence Yep.* New York: Twayne Publications, 1995.

Kovacs, Deborah, and James Preller. *Meet the Authors and Illustrators: 60 Creators of Favorite Children's Books Talk about Their Work.* Vol. 2. New York: Scholastic, 1993.

Zia, Helen, and Susan B. Gall, eds. *Notable Asian Americans.* Detroit: Gale Research, 1995.

WEB SITES

HOUGHTON MIFFLIN READING
http://www.eduplace.com/kids/hmr/mtai/yep.html
To learn more about Laurence Yep

LAURENCE YEP
http://scils.rutgers.edu/~kvander/yep.html
For information about Yep's life and work

LAURENCE YEP HOME PAGE
http://www.laurenceyep.com/
A site devoted to the author.

———

WHEN YEP WAS SEVENTEEN, A TEACHER TOLD HIS CLASS THAT TO EARN AN A THEY HAD TO GET SOMETHING PUBLISHED IN A NATIONAL MAGAZINE. THE TEACHER LATER CHANGED HIS MIND, BUT BY THEN YEP HAD ALREADY BECOME A WRITER.

Jane Yolen

Born: February 11, 1939

Jane Yolen's great grandfather was a *reb,* a storyteller, in Russia. Even as a small girl, Jane knew she had been blessed with this gift. As soon as she was able to put words down on paper, she knew she would become a writer. Today, after writing nearly 300 books of folklore, fantasy, poetry, science fiction, history, and religion—for both children and adults—new ideas still bubble to the surface faster than she can catch them.

Jane Yolen was born on February 11, 1939, in New York City. Jane's father was a newspaper writer and an international kite-flying champion. Her mother was a social worker and created crossword puzzles for maga-

---

YOLEN'S *OWL MOON* RECEIVED THE 1988 CALDECOTT MEDAL FOR ITS ILLUSTRATIONS BY JOHN SCHOENHERR.

zines. After attending high school in Connecticut, Yolen went to Smith College in Massachusetts. She returned to New York City following graduation and began working in the publishing industry.

In 1962, Yolen married a computer scientist named David Stemple. A few years later, Yolen and Stemple left their jobs and spent a year traveling through Europe and the Middle East. Everywhere she went, Yolen talked to people and learned about their lives and culture. She has tried to use their tales in her writing ever since.

> *"Folklore is the perfect second skin. From under its hide, we can see all the shimmering, shadowy uncertainties of the world."*

When Yolen and Stemple returned to the United States, they settled in a rambling farmhouse in western Massachusetts. Yolen soon gave birth to the first of her three children. She also began her full-time career as a writer, musician, storyteller, lecturer, and literary critic.

Yolen chooses her words carefully. She composes her books the way a musician writes a song. The sound of the words—their rhythm and melody—is just as important, she says, as their meaning. In fact, she never considers a piece of writing complete until she has read it out loud. She waits to be struck by a feeling that's something like love. When she feels it, she knows the work is right.

YOLEN COMPLETED *AN INVITATION TO THE BUTTERFLY BALL: A COUNTING RHYME* IN JUST THREE DAYS, BUT IT TOOK HER NINETEEN YEARS TO WRITE *THE STONE SILENUS*.

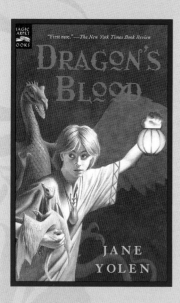

A Selected Bibliography of Yolen's Work

Dimity Duck (2006)

Baby Bear's Chairs (2005)

Flying Witch (2003)

Atalanta and the Arcadian Beast (2003)

Firebird (2002)

Girl in a Cage (2002)

Hippolyta and the Curse of the Amazons (2002)

Harvest Home (2000)

Where Have the Unicorns Gone? (2000)

Moon Ball (1999)

Armageddon Summer (1998)

The One-Armed Queen (1998)

Child of Faerie, Child of Earth (1997)

Dragon's Blood (1996)

And Twelve Chinese Acrobats (1994)

Letting Swift River Go (1992)

All Those Secrets of the World (1991)

The Devil's Arithmetic (1988)

Owl Moon (1987)

The Stone Silenus (1984)

Sleeping Ugly (1981)

Commander Toad in Space (1980)

Dream Weaver (1979)

An Invitation to the Butterfly Ball: A Counting Rhyme (1976)

The Girl Who Cried Flowers and Other Tales (1974)

The Girl Who Loved the Wind (1972)

The Emperor and the Kite (1967)

Pirates in Petticoats (1963)

Among her best-loved picture books are *Owl Moon, The Girl Who Loved the Wind,* and *Letting Swift River Go.* The stories in the Pit Dragon trilogy are high fantasy for young adults. And *The Girl Who Cried Flowers and Other Tales* brings together many of Jane Yolen's finest qualities: beautiful language, magic, originality, and a gentle handling of death, kindness, and love.

As the author of many original folk and fairy tales, Jane Yolen has been called "America's Hans Christian Andersen." As

"Ideas come from all over. It is what one does with the ideas that makes the difference."

flattering as this may be, Yolen feels it's a bit like being asked to walk in boots that are too big. She is just happy that in her long career she has been able to discover new stories, write them down, and share them with eager readers.

❧

WHERE TO FIND OUT MORE ABOUT JANE YOLEN

BOOKS

Drew, Bernard A. *The 100 Most Popular Young Adult Authors: Biographical Sketches and Bibliographies.* Englewood, Colo.: Libraries Unlimited, 1996.

McElmeel, Sharron L. *100 Most Popular Children's Authors: Biographical Sketches and Bibliographies.* Englewood, Colo.: Libraries Unlimited, 1999.

Roginski, James W. *Behind the Covers: Interviews with Authors and Illustrators of Books for Children and Young Adults.* Englewood, Colo.: Libraries Unlimited, 1985.

Something about the Author. Vol. 75. Detroit: Gale Research, 1994.

WEB SITES

INTERNET PUBLIC LIBRARY: JANE YOLEN *http://www.ipl.org/div/kidspace/askauthor/Yolen.html* For a biography of Jane Yolen and frequently asked questions

JANE YOLEN HOME PAGE *http://www.janeyolen.com/* For more information about Jane Yolen's work

---

YOLEN'S TALENT WAS RECOGNIZED EARLY, AT LEAST BY HER CLASSMATES AND TEACHER. TO THEM, SHE BECAME FAMOUS AFTER WRITING THE CLASS MUSICAL ABOUT TALKING VEGETABLES. YOLEN PLAYED THE ROLE OF A CARROT.

Ed Young

Born: November 28, 1931

When Ed Young was a student, his mother was not sure he would ever be successful. He did not get very good grades in school. Instead, he would daydream and think about drawing pictures and becoming an artist. Young went on to become a successful writer and illustrator of children's books. His best-known books include *High on a Hill: A Book of Chinese Riddles, Lon Po Po: A Red-Riding Hood Story from China,* and *Cat and Rat: The Legend of the Chinese Zodiac.* Young has also illustrated many books for other authors.

Ed Young was born on November 28, 1931, in Tientsin, China. When he was about three years old, he and his family moved to Shanghai, a much larger city. European countries controlled the area where Ed lived, so it was difficult for his family to buy the things they needed. But Ed's parents

---

ALONG WITH WORKING AS A CHILDREN'S BOOK ILLUSTRATOR, YOUNG HAS
TAUGHT ART AT SEVERAL ART SCHOOLS AND UNIVERSITIES.

worked hard and provided a comfortable life for their family.

From an early age, Ed loved to create stories and draw pictures. He often showed his drawings to friends of the family. Many people were impressed with Ed's talent, and they thought he should be an artist. But his father wanted him to study architecture.

Ed Young went to Hong Kong to finish high school. About two and a half years later, he came to the United States to attend college and study architecture. After about three years, Young realized he had made a mistake. He loved art, and so he decided to attend an art school. He finished art school three years later and

A Selected Bibliography of Young's Work

My Mei Mei (2006)

Beyond the Great Mountains (2005)

Sons of the Dragon: A Chinese Legend (2004)

What about Me? (2002)

Monkey King (2001)

The Hunter: A Chinese Folktale (Illustrations only, 2000)

White Wave: A Chinese Tale (Illustrations only, 1996)

Cat and Rat: The Legend of the Chinese Zodiac (1995)

Seven Blind Mice (Illustrations and retelling, 1992)

While I Sleep (Illustrations only, 1992)

Lon Po Po: A Red-Riding Hood Story from China (Illustrations and translation, 1989)

In the Night, Still Dark (Illustrations only, 1988)

Foolish Rabbit's Big Mistake (Illustrations only, 1985)

The Double Life of Pocahontas (Illustrations only, 1983)

Yeh-Shen: A Cinderella Story from China (Illustrations only, 1982)

High on a Hill: A Book of Chinese Riddles (1980)

Tales from the Arabian Nights (Illustrations only, 1978)

The Emperor and the Kite (Illustrations only, 1967)

The Mean Mouse and Other Mean Stories (Illustrations only, 1962)

Young's Major Literary Awards

1993 Caldecott Honor Book
1992 Boston Globe–Horn Book Picture Book Award
    Seven Blind Mice

1990 Boston Globe–Horn Book Picture Book Award
1990 Caldecott Medal
    Lon Po Po: A Red-Riding Hood Story from China

1984 Boston Globe–Horn Book Nonfiction Award
    The Double Life of Pocahontas

1983 Boston Globe–Horn Book Picture Book Honor Book
    Yeh-Shen: A Cinderella Story from China

1968 Caldecott Honor Book
    The Emperor and the Kite

moved to New York City to become an illustrator.

Young's first job was with an advertising agency. During his lunch breaks, he sketched animals at a nearby zoo. He ended up with a large collection of illustrations.

> *"A Chinese painting is often accompanied by words. They are complementary. There are things that words do that pictures never can, and likewise, there are images that words can never describe."*

When the advertising agency went out of business, Young's friends suggested that he become an illustrator for children's books. He showed his drawings to a publisher, and he was hired to illustrate *The Mean Mouse and Other Mean Stories,* written by Janice Udry. The book was published in 1962. Since then, he

> *"Before I am involved with a project, I must be moved, and as I grow, I try to create something exciting. It is my purpose to stimulate growth in the reader as an active participant."*

has done the illustrations for many other books by Jane Yolen, Jean Fritz, and Al-Ling Louie, among others.

In addition to illustrating books, Young has written his own children's books, some of which are retellings of folktales or fables. Many Chinese folktales and stories that he has retold are ones he

YOUNG OFTEN TRAVELS TO DO RESEARCH ON ANIMALS HE IS ILLUSTRATING. HE BELIEVES THAT IT IS IMPORTANT TO SEE THE ANIMALS IN THEIR OWN ENVIRONMENT, TO WATCH THEM MOVE, AND TO HEAR THE SOUNDS THEY MAKE.

remembers hearing as a child. Young does a lot of research on these folktales to make sure they are accurate.

Young lives with his family in Hastings-on-Hudson, New York. He visits China frequently to see relatives who still live there, and he continues to write and illustrate children's books.

✑

Where to Find Out More about Ed Young

Books

Marantz, Sylvia S. *Artists of the Page: Interviews with Children's Book Illustrators.* Jefferson, N.C.: McFarland, 1992.

McElmeel, Sharron L. *100 Most Popular Picture Book Authors and Illustrators: Biographical Sketches and Bibliographies.* Englewood, Colo.: Libraries Unlimited, 2000.

Rockman, Connie C., ed. *The Ninth Book of Junior Authors and Illustrators.* New York: H. W. Wilson Company, 2004.

Silvey, Anita, ed. *The Essential Guide to Children's Books and Their Creators.* Boston: Houghton Mifflin Company, 2002.

Something about the Author. Vol. 74. Detroit: Gale Research, 1993.

Web Sites

NATIONAL CENTER FOR CHILDREN'S ILLUSTRATED LITERATURE
http://www.nccil.org/young.html
To read a biography of Ed Young and a critical essay about his work

SCHOLASTIC BOOKS
http://books.scholastic.com/teachers/authorsandbooks/authorstudies/authorhome. jsp?authorID=216&displayName=Biography
For a biography about Ed Young

———

IN SCHOOL, ED YOUNG DIDN'T ALWAYS BRING HOME GOOD GRADES. HE STILL REMEMBERS HIS MOTHER WORRYING ABOUT WHAT HE WOULD DO WITH HIS LIFE.

Paul O. Zelinsky

Born: February 14, 1953

Paul O. Zelinsky published his first piece of artwork in *Highlights* magazine in 1957—when he was still in nursery school! It was just the first of many honors this amazingly talented artist has earned during his career as a book illustrator.

Paul O. Zelinsky was born in Evanston, Illinois, on February 14, 1953. His father taught college mathematics, his mother illustrated medical books, and young Paul drew. Because his father taught at several different colleges, the family moved around during Paul's childhood. Though Paul frequently had to change schools and get used to new towns, his love of drawing always stayed the same.

Although he loved art, Paul never thought about becoming an illustrator when he grew up. Instead, he imagined himself as a ventriloquist, an architect, or perhaps a teacher of natural history. It

WHEN ZELINSKY ILLUSTRATED *THE STORY OF MRS. LOVEWRIGHT AND PURRLESS HER CAT,* HE SAW THE BOOK AS HAVING "A TANGY QUALITY." HE CAPTURED THAT TANGINESS BY THINKING OF A DILL PICKLE.

wasn't until Zelinsky went to Yale University and took a course taught by

Maurice Sendak, the writer and illustrator of *Where the Wild Things Are,*

that he realized he might enjoy a
career illustrating children's books.

It didn't happen right away.
Zelinsky did a few illustrations for
the *New York Times,* went on to
get a master's degree in painting,

"I try to make the book talk, as it talks to me, and not worry whether it is in my style or not. . . . I get a kick out of doing each book differently."

and tried teaching. He admits, "I was a lousy teacher." Finally, in 1978,

he illustrated his first children's book, Avi's *Emily Upham's Revenge: A*

Massachusetts Adventure. Three years later, Zelinsky wrote and illustrated

his own book, *The Maid and the Mouse and the Odd-Shape House: A*

Story in Rhyme.

Since then, Zelinsky has written or illustrated several additional

books for young readers. His work is known for its richness, humor, and

variety. No two books are ever alike. As he himself says, "I've recently

decided that I should be recognized by my unrecognizability."

The children who pore over his books and the adults who hand out

awards don't seem to mind this "unrecognizability." Zelinsky has illustrat-

ed classic fairy tales such as *Rumpelstiltskin* and *Rapunzel,* tall tales such

as *Swamp Angel,* realistic books such as *Dear Mr. Henshaw,* fantasies such

WHEN ZELINSKY WAS WORKING ON BEVERLY CLEARY'S *RALPH S. MOUSE,*
HE VISITED A CLASSROOM TO SEE HOW REAL FIFTH-GRADERS LOOKED AND ACTED.
AND HE BOUGHT TWO MICE TO SEE HOW REAL MICE LOOKED AND ACTED.

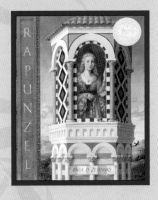

A Selected Bibliography of Zelinsky's Work

Shivers in the Fridge (Illustrations only, 2006)

Doodler Doodling (Illustrations only, 2004)

Knick-Knack Paddywhack! (2002)

Wet Magic (2001)

Awful Ogre's Awful Day (Illustrations only, 2000)

The Magic City (Illustrations only, 2000)

Five Children and It (Illustrations only, 1999)

Rapunzel (Illustrations only, 1997)

Swamp Angel (Illustrations only, 1994)

The Enchanted Castle (Illustrations only, 1992)

The Wheels on the Bus (Illustrations only, 1990)

Rumpelstiltskin (Illustrations only, 1986)

The Story of Mrs. Lovewright and Purrless Her Cat (Illustrations only, 1985)

Hansel and Gretel (Illustrations only, 1984)

Dear Mr. Henshaw (Illustrations only, 1983)

Ralph S. Mouse (Illustrations only, 1982)

The Maid and the Mouse and the Odd-Shape House: A Story in Rhyme (1981)

How I Hunted the Little Fellows (Illustrations only, 1979)

Emily Upham's Revenge: A Massachusetts Adventure (Illustrations only, 1978)

Zelinsky's Major Literary Awards

1998 Caldecott Medal
   Rapunzel

1995 Boston Globe–Horn Book Picture Book Honor Book
1995 Caldecott Honor Book
   Swamp Angel

1987 Caldecott Honor Book
   Rumpelstiltskin

1985 Caldecott Honor Book
   Hansel and Gretel

as *The Magic City,* picture books such as the gruesomely funny *Awful Ogre's Awful Day,* and the famous pop-up entitled *The Wheels on the Bus.* The list goes on and on. Sometimes Zelinsky's artwork looks as if it belongs in an art museum. Sometimes it looks like rustic folk art. And sometimes it's as bright and funny and modern as a ten-year-old kid's art.

Paul O. Zelinsky has won just about every award given for children's book illustration. *Hansel and Gretel, Rumpelstiltskin,* and *Swamp Angel* were all named Caldecott Honor Books, and in 1998, *Rapunzel* was awarded the Caldecott Medal.

Paul O. Zelinsky lives in Brooklyn, New York, with his wife, Deborah. He has two daughters—Anna and Rachel—and many more creative ideas waiting to come to life.

"It's a great deal of fun, this work. I learn things. I make things. And I feel I get to change my mind all the time about what I want to do."

❧

WHERE TO FIND OUT MORE ABOUT PAUL O. ZELINSKY

BOOKS

Cummings, Pat. *Talking With Artists, Vol. 3: Conversations with Peter Catalanotto, Raul Colon, Lisa Desimini, Jane Dyer, Kevin Hawkes, G. Brian Karas, Betsy Lewin, Ted Lewin, Keiko Narahashi, Elise Primavera, Anna Rich, Peter Sis and Paul O. Zelinsky.* Boston: Houghton Mifflin, 1999.

Holtze, Sally Holmes, ed. *Sixth Book of Junior Authors & Illustrators.* New York: H. W. Wilson Company, 1989.

WEB SITES

AUTOBIOGRAPHY FROM CHILDREN'S BOOK COUNCIL
http://www.cbcbooks.org/cbcmagazine/meet/pozelinsky.html
To read what Zelinsky says about his version of *Rumpelstiltskin*

PAUL O. ZELINSKY HOME PAGE
http://www.paulozelinsky.com/
To find out information about the author and his works

IN THEIR YOUTH, ZELINSKY AND A FRIEND TRIED TO PUBLISH A BOOK ABOUT AN ALIEN APE WHO SAVES THE WORLD FROM EVIL GORILLAS. NO ONE WAS INTERESTED IN PUBLISHING THE FANTASTIC TALE.

Margot Zemach

Born: November 30, 1931
Died: May 21, 1989

As an author and illustrator, Margot Zemach is best known and loved for bringing classic folktales to life. Her dozens of illustrated books are animated with movement and vibrant colors.

Margot Zemach was born in Los Angeles, California, in 1931. Her father was a theater director, and her mother was an actress. Even as a child, when she was first learning to draw, Margot drew illustrations of her favorite fairy tales.

With both parents working in the theater, Margot spent a lot of time backstage. She played with actors' costumes and soon began to draw dancers in lively, colorful scenes. Later, as a book illustrator, she thought of her drawings as grand stage productions. She once commented that, when illustrating a book, "I can create my own theater and be in charge of everything."

Margot studied art at several schools in Los Angeles—the Los Angeles County Art Institute, Jepson Institute of Art, Otis Art

---

ZEMACH'S STORY *EATING UP GLADYS* WAS PUBLISHED IN **2005**, MANY YEARS AFTER HER DEATH. ZEMACH'S DAUGHTER KAETHE, WHO FOUND THE STORY AMONG HER MOTHER'S PAPERS, PROVIDED THE ILLUSTRATIONS.

Institute, Kahn Art Institute, and Chouinard Art Institute. In 1955, Zemach was awarded a Fulbright scholarship, which enabled her to study overseas. She chose to attend the Vienna Academy of Fine Arts in Austria.

While in Vienna, she met another Fulbright scholar, Harvey Fischtrom. They were married in 1957, and they made their way through Europe, living for a time in Italy, Denmark, and England. They also began a long-time collaboration as an author-and-illustrator team. Their first book, published in 1959, was *A Small Boy Is Listening*. Harvey, writing under the name Harve Zemach, wrote the text, and Margot drew the illustrations.

A Selected Bibliography of Zemach's Work

Eating Up Gladys (Text only, 2005)

Some from the Moon, Some from the Sun: Poems and Songs for Everyone (2001)

Mother Goose Picture Book (1995)

Shrewd Todie and Lyzer the Miser (Illustrations only, 1994)

All God's Critters Got a Place in the Choir (Illustrations only, 1989)

Chinese Mirror (Illustrations only, 1988)

The Two Foolish Cats: Suggested by a Japanese Folktale (Illustrations only, 1987)

Three Wishes: An Old Story (1986)

Sign in Mendel's Window (Illustrations only, 1985)

Little Red Hen: An Old Story (1983)

Cat's Elbow and Other Secret Languages (Illustrations only, 1982)

Self-Portrait: Margot Zemach (1978)

To Hilda for Helping (1977)

Hush, Little Baby (1976)

It Could Always Be Worse: A Yiddish Folk Tale (1976)

The Princess and Froggie (Illustrations only, 1975)

Duffy and the Devil (Illustrations only, 1973)

Favorite Fairy Tales Told in Denmark (Illustrations only, 1971)

Awake and Dreaming (Illustrations only, 1970)

The Judge: An Untrue Tale (Illustrations only, 1969)

When Shlemiel Went to Warsaw (Illustrations only, 1968)

Too Much Nose: An Italian Tale (Illustrations only, 1967)

Fisherman and His Wife: A Tale from the Brothers Grimm (Illustrations only, 1966)

Mommy, Buy Me a China Doll: Adapted from an Ozark Children's Song (Illustrations only, 1966)

Little Tiny Woman (1965)

Salt: A Russian Tale (Illustrations only, 1965)

Three Sillies (1963)

A Small Boy Is Listening (Illustrations only, 1959)

Zemach's Major Literary Awards

1979 Boston Globe–Horn Book Nonfiction Honor Book
   Self-Portrait: Margot Zemach

1978 Caldecott Honor Book
   It Could Always Be Worse: A Yiddish Folktale

1974 Caldecott Medal
   Duffy and the Devil

1970 Caldecott Honor Book
   The Judge: An Untrue Tale

> *"When there is a story I want to tell in pictures, I find my actors, build the sets, design the costumes, and light the stage."*

The couple eventually settled in London, England, and had four daughters—Kaethe, Heidi, Rachel, and Rebecca. The family later moved to Boston, Massachusetts, and then to Berkeley, California. For the Zemachs, family life and work life were closely intertwined. The Zemach children usually played in the same area of their home where their parents worked.

Zemach went on to illustrate almost fifty children's books, many of which she wrote herself or adapted from traditional tales. She especially enjoyed illustrating stories from around the world. Among her books are folktales from England, Sweden, Denmark, Russia, Japan, Italy, and Germany.

Some of Zemach's best-loved books were adapted by her husband from traditional folktales. These include *Salt: A Russian Tale* and *Duffy and the Devil*. When the Zemachs' daughter Kaethe was fourteen, she and her father joined together to write *The Princess and Froggie*, which her mother then illustrated.

Zemach also drew the illustrations for several tales by author Isaac Bashevis Singer. He had originally written them in Yiddish, the language of the Eastern European Jewish people. Other international

---

ZEMACH PUBLISHED HER AUTOBIOGRAPHY—*SELF-PORTRAIT: MARGOT ZEMACH*—IN 1978.

stories Zemach illustrated include Virginia
Haviland's *Favorite Fairy Tales Told in
Denmark* and Yoshiko Uchida's Japanese
folktale *The Two Foolish Cats.*

Zemach died in Berkeley, California,
at the age of fifty-seven.

> *"Children are fascinated by
> detail. . . . Children need detail,
> color, excellence—the best a
> person can do."*

WHERE TO FIND OUT MORE ABOUT MARGOT ZEMACH

BOOKS

De Montreville, Doris, and Donna Hill, eds. *Third Book of Junior Authors.*
New York: H. W. Wilson, 1972.

McElmeel, Sharron L. *100 Most Popular Picture Book Authors and Illustrators: Biographical
Sketches and Bibliographies.* Englewood, Colo.: Libraries Unlimited, 2000.

Silvey, Anita, ed. *The Essential Guide to Children's Books and Their Creators.*
Boston: Houghton Mifflin Company, 2002.

Zemach, Margot. *Self-Portrait: Margot Zemach.* Reading, Mass.: Addison-Wesley, 1978.

WEB SITES

ENCYCLOPAEDIA BRITANNICA
http://www.britannica.com/ebi/article-9341076
To read a biography

PUBLISHERS WEEKLY
http://www.publishersweekly.com/article/CA6282724.html
To read Kaethe's, one of Zemach's daughters, discussion of her
mother's last book, published posthumously

THE ZEMACHS' FIRST BOOK, *A SMALL BOY IS LISTENING*, IS BASED ON THE
MUSICAL LIFE OF VIENNA, AUSTRIA, WHERE THEY HAD MET AS STUDENTS.

Paul Zindel

Born: May 15, 1936
Died: March 27, 2003

Writing stories about teenagers came naturally to Paul Zindel. Few people could match his ability to write from a teen's point of view with honesty and humor. His novels have helped to create a special category of literature, young-adult fiction. In addition to his books for young adults, Paul Zindel also wrote several renowned plays. Zindel began his novels with real, specific moments from his own life.

He made his characters believable by putting a piece of himself into each of them. In his work, readers can meet some of the people and touch on events from Zindel's own troubled childhood. They also learn the lessons that he had learned.

Paul Zindel was born on May 15, 1936, on Staten Island, New York. His father deserted the family when Paul was only two. His mother often moved with Paul and his sister, looking for work.

ZINDEL ENJOYED READING WORKS BY OTHER YOUNG-ADULT WRITERS, INCLUDING PAULA DANZIGER, PATRICIA MACLACHLAN, AND LIZ LEVY.

As a result, Paul never had close friends and spent much of his time alone. But he had an active imagination and found ways to entertain himself with puppets, comic books, and movies.

In high school, Paul began writing plays. His interest in theater continued to grow in college. At Wagner College on Staten Island, Zindel took a course taught by playwright Edward Albee, who had a great influence on his writing.

After graduating with a chemistry degree, Zindel began teaching chemistry and physics at Tottenville High School on Staten Island.

In his spare time, Zindel continued to write plays, including *The Effect of Gamma Rays*

A Selected Bibliography of Zindel's Work

Death on the Amazon (2002)
The Gadget (2001)
Night of the Bat (2001)
Rats (1999)
Reef of Death (1998)
The Doom Stone (1995)
David & Della (1993)
Fifth Grade Safari (1993)
The Pigman & Me (1991)
A Begonia for Miss Applebaum (1989)
The Amazing and Death-Defying Diary of Eugene Dingman (1987)
Harry and Hortense at Hormone High (1984)
The Girl Who Wanted a Boy (1981)
The Pigman's Legacy (1980)
The Undertaker's Gone Bananas (1978)
Confessions of a Teenage Baboon (1977)
Pardon Me, You're Stepping on My Eyeball! (1976)
I Love My Mother (1975)
Let Me Hear You Whisper (1974)
The Secret Affairs of Margaret Wild (1973)
The Effect of Gamma Rays on Man-in-the-Moon Marigolds (1971)
I Never Loved Your Mind (1970)
My Darling, My Hamburger (1969)
The Pigman (1968)

Zindel's Major Literary Award

1969 Boston Globe-Horn Book Fiction Honor Book
   The Pigman

> *"I like storytelling. We all have an active thing that we do that gives us self-esteem, that makes us proud; it's necessary. I have to tell stories because that's the way the wiring went in."*

on *Man-in-the-Moon Marigolds* in 1963. The play opened on Broadway in 1971 and won many awards, including an Obie Award, a New York Drama Critics' Circle Award, and the Pulitzer Prize.

Zindel's first and best-known novel is *The Pigman,* published in 1968. It is based on a common Zindel theme: troubled teenagers befriending adults. Through tragedy, the teens learn about themselves and how to cope with life and death.

A year after Zindel published his first novel, he quit teaching. He believed that he could do more for teenagers as a writer than as a teacher. In 1973, he married Bonnie Hildebrand. They had two children, David Jack and Elizabeth Claire.

Writing kept Paul Zindel very busy. In addition to his many young-adult novels, he

> *"I like to write for kids about worlds they can identify with—worlds they know that they're interested in and worlds that have characters who are solving problems that they themselves would want to solve."*

wrote a children's book, a series of books for middle-grade readers (the

ZINDEL WORKED AS A WAITER, A BARTENDER, A DANCE INSTRUCTOR, A CHEMIST, A CHIMNEY SWEEP, AND A TECHNICAL WRITER.

Wacky Facts Lunch Bunch series), and several plays and movie screen-plays. His work brings humor and hope to people struggling to make sense of life. He offers teens a different view of the world and gives them meaning as they journey through it. Zindel's message is clear: "It is glorious to be young and to be involved in the great adventure of life." Zindel died March 27, 2003.

⋆

WHERE TO FIND OUT MORE ABOUT PAUL ZINDEL

BOOKS
Drew, Bernard A. *The 100 Most Popular Young Adult Authors: Biographical Sketches and Bibliographies.* Englewood, Colo.: Libraries Unlimited, 1997.

Hedblad, Alan, ed. *Something about the Author.* Vol. 102. Detroit: Gale Research, 1999.

Silvey, Anita, ed. *The Essential Guide to Children's Books and Their Creators.* Boston: Houghton Mifflin Company, 2002.

Zindel, Paul. *The Pigman and Me.* New York: HarperCollins, 1992.

WEB SITES
RANDOM HOUSE
http://www.randomhouse.com/teachers/authors/results.pperl?authorid=34133
For an interview with, fun facts about, and comments by Paul Zindel

SCHOLASTIC
http://books.scholastic.com/teachers/authorsandbooks/authorstudies/authorhome.jsp?authorID=217&collateralID=5312&displayName=Biography
To read a biographical sketch of Paul Zindel

———

ZINDEL KEPT A JOURNAL THAT HE USES FOR INSPIRATION. IN IT HE PUT NOTES, TAPE RECORDINGS, PHOTOS, VIDEO EXCERPTS, MOVIE STILLS, POEMS, MAGAZINE CLIPPINGS, AND NEWSPAPER ARTICLES.

Gene Zion

Born: October 5, 1913
Died: December 5, 1975

G ene Zion had what one critic called a gift for seeing a story "through the eyes of the child." His books have charmed readers for decades and will entertain young people for many years to come.

Gene Zion was born in New York City on October 5, 1913. He grew up in nearby Ridgefield, New Jersey. "Life was rural," he wrote later, "and included a barn with a cow, chickens, and pigeons." Gene started drawing in kindergarten and decided early on that he wanted to do something creative with his life.

Zion attended the New School for Social Research and the Pratt Institute in New York City. He studied advertising art, and in 1936 he designed a travel poster that won

> *"No creative effort has been more gratifying for me than writing picture books for children."*

a contest. As a result, he got to travel and live in Europe for a while. There he visited printing plants and became interested in making books.

ZION'S ORIGINAL TYPEWRITTEN MANUSCRIPTS OF HIS BOOKS STILL EXIST. THEY ARE IN THE LIBRARY AT THE UNIVERSITY OF MINNESOTA.

When World War II (1939–1945) began, Zion joined the army. His job was to design training manuals and filmstrips to teach soldiers in the antiaircraft artillery. After the war, he worked for the CBS radio network and for several magazine publishers. Eventually, he became a freelance designer.

By this time, Zion had married artist and illustrator Margaret Bloy Graham. Graham and the great children's book editor Ursula Nordstrom persuaded Zion to try writing a picture book. Zion looked at a sketch his wife had made years before of children gathering apples in an orchard. It gave him the idea for *All Falling Down*, his first book.

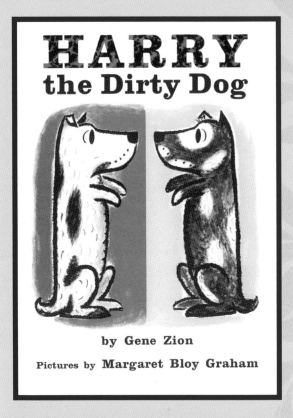

A Selected Bibliography of Zion's Work

Harry by the Sea (1965)
The Sugar Mouse Cake (1964)
The Meanest Squirrel I Ever Met (1962)
Harry and the Lady Next Door (1960)
The Plant Sitter (1959)
No Roses for Harry (1958)
Dear Garbage Man (1957)
Jeffie's Party (1957)
Harry the Dirty Dog (1956)
Really Spring (1956)
Summer Snowman (1955)
Hide and Seek Day (1954)
All Falling Down (1951)

The story, like all of Zion's stories, is very simple. It is hardly more than a list of things that fall down, such as apples, leaves, and snow. The book, which included illustrations by Graham, was very successful, however.

Zion and Graham worked together on thirteen books. Their best-known books are about Harry the Dog. The first was *Harry the Dirty Dog*, in which Harry, a white dog with black spots, gets so dirty that he becomes a black dog with white spots. His owners don't even recognize him until Harry breaks down and takes a bath. Harry is portrayed in few words and through simple pictures, but he is a memorable character, and his books have been popular ever since.

Zion and Graham wrote four Harry the Dog books. The last was *Harry by the Sea*, published in 1965, in which Harry gets lost at the beach. When he returns, he's a mess again and looks like a creature made of seaweed.

> *"Harry was a white dog with black spots who liked everything, except . . . getting a bath."*
> —*Harry the Dirty Dog*

Zion and Margaret Bloy Graham divorced in 1968. Zion died on December 5, 1975. Almost five decades after its publication, his *Harry the Dirty Dog* is still in print.

HARRY THE DIRTY DOG HAS BEEN ADAPTED FOR A NUMBER OF CHILDREN'S THEATER PRODUCTIONS.

❧

WHERE TO FIND OUT MORE ABOUT GENE ZION

BOOK

Fuller, Muriel, ed. *More Junior Authors.*
New York: H. W. Wilson Company, 1963.

WEB SITES

HARPER COLLINS

http://www.harpercollinschildrens.com/HarperChildrens/
Kids/AuthorsAndIllustrators/ContributorDetail.aspx?CId=12950
For a short biography of Zion

UNIVERSITY OF MINNESOTA LIBRARIES

http://special.lib.umn.edu/findaid/html/clrc/clrc0201.html
To read a short biography of Zion

———

ZION FIRST WORKED AS A PROFESSIONAL ARTIST WHEN HE WAS A
SCHOOLBOY. HIS FRIENDS USED TO PAY HIM TO PAINT PICTURES
ON THE BACK OF THEIR YELLOW RAIN SLICKERS.

Charlotte Zolotow

Born: June 26, 1915

Charlotte Zolotow enjoyed a long career as an editor of children's books. She is also the author of dozens of picture books for young children. Her many troubling childhood experiences made her determined to write about life from a child's point of view.

Zolotow was born Charlotte Shapiro in Norfolk, Virginia, in 1915. Even before she started school, she enjoyed reading and drawing pictures. She would tell people that she wanted to be a writer and illustrator when she grew up.

Charlotte and her older sister, Dorothy, lived in many cities as their father moved around for business reasons. Charlotte was shy and had trouble fitting in at new schools. In addition, she wore glasses,

IN 1998, THE COOPERATIVE CHILDREN'S BOOK CENTER AT THE UNIVERSITY OF WISCONSIN IN MADISON CREATED THE CHARLOTTE ZOLOTOW AWARD. THIS ANNUAL AWARD HONORS THE AUTHOR OF A DISTINGUISHED PICTURE BOOK WITH A CASH PRIZE AND A GOLD MEDAL.

braces on her teeth, and a back brace for curvature of the spine. In her misery, Charlotte withdrew into writing. In third grade, she wrote a story about her family pet. Later, another story she wrote was published in *The American Girl* magazine.

When the family moved to New York City, Charlotte's new school had more students than she had ever encountered. The stress of the crowd gave her fainting spells, so she was put into a small, private school. When a teacher there complimented Charlotte on her writing skills, she was even more determined to be a writer.

"Children have the same emotions as adults, though they experience them more intensely, since they haven't yet learned the protective camouflage with which we adults disguise our feelings."

In 1933, Charlotte won a writing scholarship to the University of Wisconsin in Madison. There she met another writing student, Maurice Zolotow, and they married in 1938. They later had two children—Stephen and Ellen.

The couple moved to New York City, where Zolotow went to work for Harper & Brothers publishing company. (The company's name later changed to Harper & Row and then became HarperCollins.) Zolotow eventually was promoted to senior editor in the children's book department.

ZOLOTOW'S DAUGHTER, WHO CHANGED HER NAME TO CRESCENT DRAGONWAGON, IS ALSO A CHILDREN'S BOOK AUTHOR.

A Selected Bibliography of Zolotow's Work

The Moon Was the Best (1993)

This Quiet Lady (1992)

The Seashore Book (1992)

If You Listen (1980)

It's Not Fair (1976)

My Grandson Lew (1974)

William's Doll (1972)

Wake Up and Goodnight (1971)

Summer Is . . . (1967)

If It Weren't for You (1966)

Someday (1965)

The Sky Was Blue (1963)

The White Marble (1963)

Mr. Rabbit and the Lovely Present (1962)

Do You Know What I'll Do? (1958)

The Sleepy Book (1958)

Indian, Indian (1952)

The Storm Book (1952)

But Not Billy (1947)

The Park Book (1944)

The Zolotows' apartment overlooked Washington Square Park in New York City's Greenwich Village neighborhood. Zolotow thought the activities in the park would be a great subject for one of her company's authors to write about. But her boss thought Zolotow herself should write the book. In 1944, it was published as *The Park Book*.

Zolotow went on to excel as both an editor and an author. As an editor, she launched the careers of many excellent children's book authors. In 1981, HarperCollins created a division called Charlotte Zolotow Books. Zolotow remained its editorial director until 1991.

As an author, Zolotow is noted for her simple, touching

stories that show a child's viewpoint. In *Mr. Rabbit and the Lovely Present*, a girl and her friend—a large bunny—search for the perfect gift for her mother. *My Grandson Lew* was one of the first children's books to deal with death. It portrays a young boy grieving for his grandfather who has died.

William's Doll caused a bit of commotion when it was first published in 1972. It's about a little boy who enjoys his basketball and electric train, but he also wants a doll to hug and care for. The boy's father is not pleased, but Zolotow resolves this dilemma gracefully and tastefully.

Zolotow currently lives in Hastings-on-Hudson, New York.

> *"Most of my books are about the ordinary, daily relationships between children and adults, brothers and sisters . . . and the infinite variety of personal encounters out of which emotions arise."*

❧

WHERE TO FIND OUT MORE ABOUT CHARLOTTE ZOLOTOW

WEB SITES
HARPER COLLINS
http://www.harpercollins.com/authors/12952/Charlotte_Zolotow/index.aspx
For an interview and biographical information

THE OFFICIAL CHARLOTTE ZOLOTOW WEB SITE
http://www.charlottezolotow.com
To learn about Zolotow's life and work

___

ZOLOTOW HAS WRITTEN SEVERAL BOOKS OF POETRY FOR CHILDREN.

INDEX

G